Scott Gooding is a cook and a holistic nutrition and performance coach. **Matilda Brown** is best known for her work as a writer, director and actress. The two are advocates for regenerative agriculture, and together opened The Good Farm Shop in 2021. Based in Sydney's Brookvale, the shop has transformed from a small online butchery to a ready-meals company that delivers across the east coast of Australia. The couple have three children and split their time between their home on Sydney's northern beaches and Matilda's family's farm in Nambucca Valley on the Mid North Coast of New South Wales.

The Good Farm Cookbook

It started with an email to family and friends
asking if anyone wanted to go in on a cow
share. We wanted to eat the meat from our farm,
knowing that we were taking care of the land
and providing a lovely life for the animals.
But logistically, it's hard to get that cow on
your plate. And our local butcher, much like
yours probably, didn't know where his meat
came from either. This sparked our interest
in food sovereignty and started us on the path
to building our business. The recipes in this
book embody all that we have learnt about food,
recently and over our lifetimes.

The Good Farm Cookbook

EVERYDAY FAMILY RECIPES FOR A NOURISHING, HOPEFUL LIFE

Scott Gooding + Matilda Brown

murdoch books

Sydney | London

CONTENTS

How and why our food choices matter

SCOTT

I don't remember when exactly I began to care about where the food on my plate came from. For as long as I can remember, I've wanted to buy animal products of the highest quality, not from a flavour perspective necessarily but from an ethical one. It's simply a personal non-negotiable. I would rather go without eggs than buy the caged variety. In my first cookbook in 2013 I talked about food sovereignty (taking back control of the production of food) in an attempt to raise awareness of this topic. But in 2021 I literally made it my business to care. This was when Til and I set up The Good Farm Shop, first as a butchery, then a ready-meals producer, and with food sovereignty at its centre. Til and I personally know every one of our farmer suppliers and how they manage their animals and land.

In most parts of the world, we have gotten ourselves into a real pickle with food and, more specifically, our system of food production – the industrialised food system. In some weird way we have adopted an imperialistic view of nature, like we own it and can do what we want with it.

For thousands of years, we relied exclusively on manual inputs or the work of animals such as oxen, horses and mules to farm our land. But in the early twentieth century this began to change. The mechanisation of agriculture reduced the need for manual labour, and an all-out race began to industrialise farming to maximise yields. This paved the way for large areas of land to be singularly devoted to one species of crop (mono-cropping), which led to widespread use of herbicides and pesticides. Our food production became highly commoditised, including the way we breed and raise animals. (Just look up industrialised pig farming, feedlots, battery hens and rumen fistulas and you'll find some confronting images.) The outcome of this approach is not pretty. No one wins. The animal has a less-than-ordinary life, the local ecology takes a hit from mono-cropping, and generations of people inherit the cost of both these things.

The upside? We have incredible access to food: walk into any supermarket and you'll see wall-to-wall produce. Shelves are replenished daily and items are rarely out of stock. In some ways, it's a great time to be alive – all that choice and abundance! But the downside is that we readily fill our baskets with little consideration for where the products have come from, and for decades that hasn't really mattered. We have inherited the legacy of unconscious food consumption that has prevailed for most of the past fifty years.

People are gradually realising that industrialised agriculture is not the only option. It is possible to shop and consume plants and animal products in a way that supports better animal husbandry and a healthy ecosystem. There is an emerging and growing community of consumers and producers who are prepared to question where their food comes from, and we are proud to be a part of this.

You could try it too. Ask your fishmonger, your butcher and even your supermarket where the food comes from. Admittedly, it is harder at the supermarket to connect with someone who knows, but the more we try, the more they register it as an issue. You might be pleasantly surprised that the steak you've been buying for years from your local store is ethically raised, grass finished, free of chemicals and grown locally.

But what if it's not ... ?

For the sake of animal welfare, soil health, our water systems and the earth's ability to sequester carbon, it is everyone's responsibility to question the provenance of the food they put in their basket.

We can ask:

- Did the animal have a good life?
- Did it have access to the foods it would eat in nature?
- Was it free to move around as it would in nature?
- Was it subjected to hormone or antibiotic injections, or vaccines?
- Did the crop grow without chemical interventions and as part of a natural landscape?
- Was it locally produced?

The story of the farm and The Good Farm Shop

TIL

The farm has always been a part of my life. My parents bought it in 1985 when they were filming in the Nambucca Valley in New South Wales and fell in love with the area. It was the first farm they saw – a shabby weatherboard farmhouse on 250 acres. I came along in 1987, so some of my earliest and best memories are of life on the farm. Eating dippy eggs on the balcony, going to pony club, galloping through the fire trails on my horse Happy Jack with Mum beside me on hers, Dad teaching me to drive the truck, playing kick the can with the cousins. The farm was also responsible for toughening us up. Swimming in the dam meant we'd often find leeches stuck to our bodies; I'd look up from my bed to see a huge huntsman spider in the corner of the room; and red-bellied black, brown and tiger snakes were a common sight in summer. As a child, the farm was a place to run wild. As a teen, it was family time and an escape from the city. As an adult, it has been a place of solace and a writing den. And now, as a mother, I see my kids enjoying it for all the same reasons I did when I was their age.

The farm is now a working regenerative cattle farm managed by a very small team, including my mum. But it hasn't always been. It wasn't until 2019 that Mum and Mick (another local farmer and our former farm manager, pictured on page 13) started the regenerative process (see page 31 for an explanation of regen' farming and why it's important, and page 198 for more on Mum's journey to regen' farming).

And it wasn't until 2021 that Scott and I started to understand the difference between the two and really take notice. It was then that we decided we wanted to be eating meat from regenerative farms. I asked our local butcher if he sold any regen' meat, but he had no idea what I was talking about, and the supermarket sure as hell didn't sell it. So, we took matters into our own hands and started a cow-share directly from our farm. And that's how The Good Farm Shop was born.

We hadn't planned to start a business, but one cow, once a month, quickly evolved into us sourcing produce from a handful of regenerative farms across New South Wales and delivering beef, pork, lamb, duck, chicken and eggs to doorsteps across the state, as well as to Queensland and Victoria. Our customers loved the produce and the values, and our revenue was growing ... but our profit was not. We couldn't make the business work financially, at least not by buying whole animals from small regenerative farms.

Still, it would have been a shame to quit. Both Scott and I were at a crossroads. We'd said goodbye to nearly a decade of work (me as an actress, writer and director, and Scott as a health coach, trainer and ambassador for several companies) to build The Good Farm Shop. We were loving working together, and it felt good to be contributing to something positive in the world. People were grateful for what we were doing: providing them with access to food that made them feel good. Some bought from us because they were gung-ho about the environment, some were health focused and others really cared about the way animals were treated. If we were going to put all of our time into the business, we just had to find a way to ensure it was financially viable.

It was during a trip to the UK to visit Scott's family at the end of 2022 that we found a potential way forward. It's not often that you find yourself feeling inspired in a supermarket aisle, but there we were in Waitrose, encouraged and excited by how much further ahead the supermarket was with the concept of regenerative farming and food sovereignty and, most surprisingly, the quality of their ready meals. We had already been making meals from the less popular cuts of meat (primarily chuck and mince), and the feedback had been great. So, in February of 2023, we closed the butchery side of our business and extended our ready-meals line. It was a different direction, but our values and philosophy remained the same.

Within a month, we'd moved The Good Farm Shop out of its small warehouse and into a full commercial kitchen. We pivoted and rebranded the business. We continued to use regenerative animal produce from small, family-owned farms, including our own, and complemented these products with organic ingredients, and no preservatives, fillers or gluten. Australia didn't need another ordinary ready-meals business; we have plenty of those. But there was certainly room for one that prioritised caring about the environment, human health and animal welfare. And so, The Good Farm Shop was reborn, and that's what it remains today.

It's more than just a business for us, it's our creative glue. A metaphor for raising our family and tending to our wellbeing. And it mirrors our philosophy and outlook, and the way we choose to tread on the earth.

Our stories

SCOTT

My affinity with food and, in particular, my love of meat, began when I was old enough to sit in a highchair. At the time – the mid-seventies – my folks ran a pub in London, back when boozers were literally just drinking holes. They were trying to do something different: to cultivate a food-first pub culture and entice customers back with familiar, comforting and delicious dishes. Mum used to plonk me in the highchair in the kitchen while she prepped and cooked for the punters, and the kitchen staff used to throw me hunks of ham and cheese to keep me occupied.

I began cooking at a young age, largely from necessity, as my parents would nap between shifts when I got home from school. Plus, the kitchens were so busy at night I daren't add my order into the mix, piling more pressure on the cantankerous Scottish chef. I enjoyed experimenting and was lucky to have access to fridges full of fresh produce. This meant my school lunchbox smelt very different to everyone else's, the waft of prawns, pâté and liver sausage overpowering my neighbour's Marmite sandwich – uncomfortable for a teenager who just wanted to fit in.

After school I headed off to university, where alcohol became my main source of sustenance. I would drink most nights and hit it hard Thursday through to Sunday. I gained some weight, had pains in my kidneys and felt like crap much of the time. I soon realised I had to offset this destructive behaviour with exercise, so I began running.

Having an exercise science degree, I knew the principles of exercise and how to improve the markers of fitness, but I'm an all-or-nothing guy, and I trained hard and often – an unsustainable combination. If I had been eating properly (both quality and quantity) I might have passed through this period unscathed, but I was underfuelling, motivated by a thin veil of body dysmorphia. I was also living in a vegetarian household, which meant I wasn't hitting my protein needs – an essential nutrient at the best of times, but critical when loading and stressing the body with intense exercise.

When I moved to Sydney in 1999, this intense training habit was joined by a drug habit, and for the next few years I was burning the candle at both ends. Something had to give and, in the end, it was my body – a relatively minor back strain ruptured some discs in my lower back, and I spent the next seven years dealing with pain, isolation and depression.

I tried to fix my back with traditional methods: I went to physios, osteos, chiros and massage therapists, but nothing worked. It wasn't until 2012 that I considered food as a potential treatment. I systematically eliminated inflammatory foods from my diet, and became quite militant about it: out went bread, pasta, sugar, cereals, crackers … everything I understood not to be good for me. As soon as I saw results, I doubled down even harder. I became a pain-in-the-arse to cook for and it wasn't long before dinner invitations dried up. I was also a nightmare for waiters and chefs. But it was working, so I didn't care.

It was around this time I got the chance to compete on the cooking TV show *My Kitchen Rules*. It immersed me in the world of cooking again – flavour combinations, recipes, cooking under pressure, researching and practising. My experience on the show nudged me in the direction of cooking for a living and allowed me to explore the culinary landscape.

Since then, I have opened restaurants, become an holistic nutrition coach, a sports nutritionist and an exercise specialist, and written nine books on food. My earlier cookbooks prescribed adherence to strict food regimes but, the truth is, if I hadn't had a serious injury I so desperately wanted to fix, I wouldn't have felt the need to re-evaluate my diet so drastically. It sent me off on a dietary orbit that evolved over years to include fasting, ketosis and a high-protein diet, but really what all of these things did is show me the power and potency of food as a lever for health.

Over the years I've loosened up and changed my focus – I'm not a complete pain-in-the-arse about food anymore.

All of these experiences have impacted the food philosophy I have today: that nose-to-tail, wholefood and no-fuss cooking is best. Nourishing, easy, familiar and flavourful food. Essentially, my mum's cooking, version 2.0!

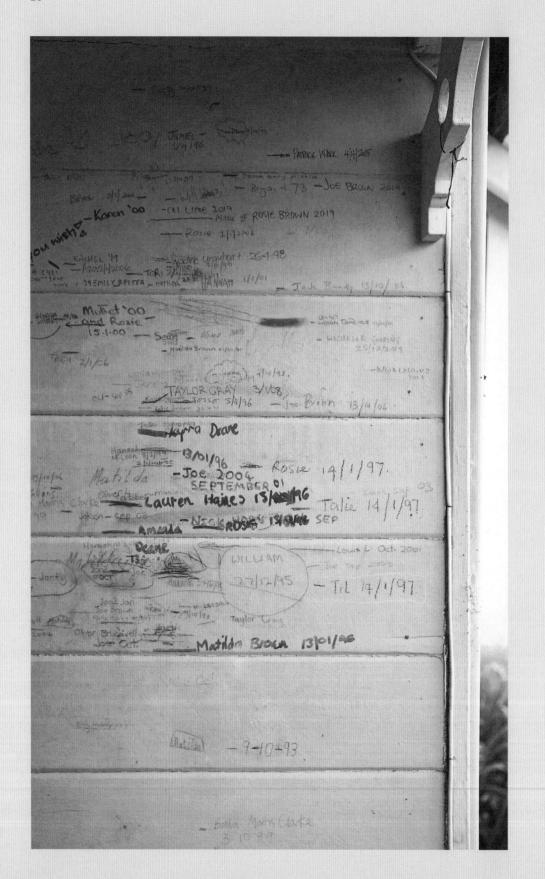

TIL

For those of you who don't know me from a bar of soap (that's 99.99 per cent of you), I'll give you a little context. I'm thirty-six, I have two kids and a stepson, and I am the co-owner of The Good Farm Shop. I am in the food industry, yes, but I haven't always been. I grew up in the film industry. My dad, Bryan Brown (pictured on pages 114–15), is an actor, producer and writer, and my mum, Rachel Ward (pictured overleaf), is an actress, writer and director. Many would call them famous but, despite their fame, they keep it very real. (In fact, I can pretty much guarantee you've never seen more of a shitbox than the car my dad drives.) My siblings and I grew up between the Northern Beaches of Sydney and the family farm. Then, when I was nine, we said goodbye to suburban beach life and moved to the big smoke. After high school, I studied film and TV, and spent most of my twenties travelling back and forth between LA and Sydney, following in my parents' footsteps. I had an amazing upbringing, and my twenties were an incredible time in my life. But the shadow of it was the ongoing struggle I had with food, eating and my weight.

In primary school, I was an athlete. I won all the school races, climbed every tree and pretty much cartwheeled my way through life. 'Fat' wasn't something I related to my body, as I didn't have an ounce to spare. I ate when I wanted, however I wanted. But when I hit puberty, everything changed. My hips grew, my tummy lost its washboard look, I got boobs (big boobs) and I started to hide under baggy clothes. My mum noticed, and, like most mums at the time, found diet upon diet for me to subscribe to, thinking she was helping. None gave me an understanding of nutrition; all they did was crowd my head with conflicting information. My weight fluctuated. I was self-conscious, anxious, ashamed. I stopped going to parties, and instead hid in my room, writing dark, soul-searching poetry. I exercised, but it made little difference. I got further and further away from the body I wanted: those of the beautiful girls on the front of magazines (thank God TikTok and Instagram weren't around then).

All through my teenage years and into my early twenties, I tried to lose weight. I'd starve myself only to binge and purge for days at a time. Then I'd feel so ashamed, I'd starve myself again, then binge and purge again. Shame. Starve. Binge. Purge. A vicious cycle. At twenty-three I discovered calorie counting and running and, for the first time ever, worked out that if I just ate less than I burnt, I could lose weight. I dropped 10 kilograms quickly, fitting neatly into a size eight. But I still knew nothing about nutrition, or how to nourish or heal my body. I just ate to be thin. Food became numbers. Bland food, like rice crackers, were easy to add up. An apple = 80 calories. A tin of tuna = 100. A slice of cheese = 30. I kept track of them in the notes section of my phone. At night, I would lay there, making sure I hadn't overeaten, terrified I'd wake up the next day back in a body I didn't want.

Being an actress didn't help. I rarely focused on the role, much more concerned with how I looked. They say the camera adds a few pounds, and through the lens of body dysmorphia, I was convinced I looked even fatter on screen. More running, fewer calories. My periods stopped, and a thin layer of hair grew over my face and arms. My head felt slow, like it wasn't getting what it needed. And then, as if that wasn't enough, I watched a bunch of documentaries on the meat industry. Now I had the perfect excuse to pretty much just eat air. 'I'm vegan', I declared to my family and friends. At twenty-five I'd finally worked out the secret to staying thin, but I panicked whenever someone invited me to lunch or dinner. I had to constantly be in control of the food I ate. I was moody and hangry most of the time. This is not how I thought being thin would feel.

That was the height of my eating disorder. At some point in my late twenties, I relaxed a little. I found a balance somewhere between a vegan and vegetarian diet, and ate predominately carbohydrates, vegetables, a small amount of soy, quinoa and quite a lot of fruit. I still exercised every day, but my metabolism felt slow. Even counting calories wasn't really working. The weight slowly crept back on. Then, I met Scott and everything changed. Aside from falling in love and knowing I'd met the man I would have a family with, I'd met someone who taught me more about nutrition in the first two months of our relationship than I'd learnt in my years of body struggle and shame. The biggest change to my diet was starting to eat meat again after seven years without it. I was a lazy vegan/vegetarian. I didn't prioritise good protein, and I didn't supplement enough. My body had suffered over the years from the lack of healthy fats, good nutrient-dense protein and being flogged to the point of exhaustion. The moment I took a bite of the slow-cooked lamb Scott made for me, I never looked back. It was like WD40 for my bones. I felt my body absorbing its goodness for days afterwards, and I've devoured meat ever since. Scott's way of eating has had a massive influence on me and turned out to be the antidote to my body's inability to find its natural, healthy weight, without deprivation. Sometimes I can't believe how simple it is, and I'm shocked it took me half a lifetime to work it out.

You might wonder if I still fall into any of my old habits. The truth is, I really don't. Calorie counting has been useful for me to understand how much energy my body needs on any given day, but I couldn't tell you the last time I counted a calorie. Some days I'm so ravenously hungry that I eat way beyond what I have physically expended, and others when I'm so busy with the kids and work, I forget or don't have time to eat until early afternoon. I have learnt to trust what my body needs more intuitively than I used to. I appreciate my body for what it is capable of far more than what it looks like, and eating the way we do means I'm never left feeling malnourished or unsatisfied. Food was once my enemy – now it is my medicine.

> Eating the way we do means
> I'm never left feeling
> malnourished or unsatisfied.
> Food was once my enemy –
> now it is my medicine.

> "There is an emerging
> and growing community
> of consumers and
> producers who are
> prepared to question
> where their food comes
> from, and we are proud
> to be a part of this.

How we eat as a family and why

SCOTT

The Gooding family is a matriarchal one. Til is most definitely at the helm in the majority of situations, but one area of our life where I do have a big influence is deciding what we eat and doing most of the cooking. It's not a dictatorship ... at least not anymore. My previously rigid stance on nutrition (see page 16) has softened. I no longer pick legumes out of my salads, chastise corn, or vilify the humble spud.

These days, we toe a consistent nutritional line that includes, by and large, eating nutrient-dense foods that are natural and unprocessed, and avoiding highly processed foods. All our kids have input and agency over their food choices. I encourage free will and individual preferences, but equally I don't run a cafe or cook to order. The little kids eat together, slightly earlier than Til, myself and Tashi, and we cook 95 per cent of our meals from scratch.

I build our meals around protein, an essential macronutrient. It's a pretty good rule of thumb to guide your meal composition. Whether you choose to eat meat or not, make protein the starting point of any meal, then build in veggies and other elements. Fat should come from animal protein and/or the oils you use for cooking, and – voila! A balanced meal and a balanced diet. I don't weigh or measure food, just base my meal choices on instincts, accumulated knowledge and preferences.

Whether it's eggs or oxtails, we buy the highest-welfare protein possible, and from producers with the best farming practices. For us, this means buying our meat from regenerative farms or local butchers who know where their meat comes from, and yes – this generally means we are paying more than we would if we bought from the supermarket. Eating meat less frequently, or using cheaper cuts and learning the best way to cook them, is a good way to make this approach more affordable. We buy organic where possible and try to follow a gluten-free diet. This enables us to raise resilient, healthy kids on delicious food while causing the least disruption or harm to nature's ecosystems.

The recipes in this book reflect where I am today, in a space where food nourishes and sustains, and brings people together. When I'm cooking for the family, I'm wearing my 'chef's hat' and my 'nutritionist's hat' simultaneously, and I believe that where these two spheres overlap is the marriage of healthy and delicious food. I'm also wearing my 'dad hat', meaning I only want the best for them – and, as contradictory as it may sound, this also means allowing some indulgences from time to time: the occasional ice cream at the beach, hot chips on a road trip, or a chocolate, just because. This includes treats for the grown-ups too; life is too short to miss out on warm sourdough with butter, an apple crumble or one of Til's margaritas …

These are the central principles we apply to our food choices and preparation for the betterment of human, animal and environmental health.
· We recommend that you use protein produced with the highest level of animal welfare when you make our recipes
· All our recipes are gluten free
· We don't use any processed foods.

The table below will help you navigate shopping with provenance in mind. The key is to become somewhat of a food detective, and slowly surround yourself with brands, growers and producers you trust. Identifying and understanding labels, nutritional claims and buzzwords will stand you in good stead, too.

BEEF	CHICKEN	EGGS	FISH	FRUIT AND VEG
Regeneratively farmed (biodynamic, holistically farmed, natural sequence etc.): Land to Market verified	Regeneratively raised (LDMO: Low Density Mobile Outdoors)	Regeneratively raised (LDMO: Low Density Mobile Outdoors)	Marine Stewardship Council (MSC) certified	Regeneratively farmed
	Free-range organic	Free-range organic	Wild (line)-caught	Organic
Organic (grass-finished)	Free range	Free range	Aquaculture Stewardship Council (ASC) farmed	Seasonal
Grass-fed/finished				

Regenerative farming and why it matters

TIL

It isn't our style to lecture about the state of the world. There are more well-equipped people for that. Neither are we here to be the bearers of bad news. We're simply on a journey to get to the core of what we believe to be the best possible food practices, and we want it to be uplifting, inspiring and energising. Not only for ourselves, but for our kids, our friends and you.

Hope, inspiration, enthusiasm ... these are words that light me up. They make me feel strong, compelled, willing to learn and, ultimately, they make me care. And I believe that once we truly care about something, action follows.

In the words of one of the greatest pioneers of regenerative farming, Zimbabwean Allan Savory:

> " I care enough
> about the land,
> the wildlife,
> people, the future
> of humanity. If you
> care enough, you
> will do whatever
> you have to do,
> no matter what
> the opposition.

Let's talk about regenerative agriculture and why it matters, from a scientific perspective. Wait, don't close the book! Amazingly, the science of regenerative agriculture is not remotely boring and is easy enough for a primary-school kid to understand. And it's important to get your head around, so stay with me.

Regenerative ('regen') agriculture is a big term, but really all it means is the improvement of the land – specifically the soil. You'd never guess it, but soil is the real hero of the story here. Soil is a living, breathing, complex, creative and intelligent community of trillions of microorganisms that nurtures plant life and aids photosynthesis. Importantly, soil also takes carbon out of our atmosphere and locks it into the ground in a process called carbon sequestration. It is this ability that gives soil its superpower status. When soil is at its best, there is no end to how much carbon it can store.

Okay, so now that you understand why soil is the hero, it's important to understand soil's kryptonite: chemicals. These come in many forms – fertilisers, pesticides, herbicides, weed killer – and you've probably got a few of them sitting in plastic containers in your garden shed right now. For decades, chemicals like these have been used in agricultural food production to eliminate pests and weeds and increase crop yields. Now, I've checked out the safety instructions for one of these products – it's a compelling read, but I'll save you the 20 minutes.

On page four of eight, it recommends covering your entire body with 'suitable work wear' and donning safety goggles or a full-face shield and thick gloves. That's quite a lot of protective gear for something that is sprayed willy-nilly onto the fields in which our fruit and veg grow.

Problem is, not only can these chemicals be harmful to human health, but they are also very harmful to soil health. They kill weeds and pests, but they also kill earthworms and other types of invertebrates, algae, honeybees and myriad microorganisms that keep soil healthy and thriving. When soil is no longer functioning normally, it can't do its job: to grow nutrient-rich crops, aid photosynthesis and capture and store carbon. For many decades, conventional farming has relied on the heavy use of chemicals, to the point where the health of our soil has significantly degraded. Chemicals deplete the microbiome of the soil so that the only way back is through the use of fertilisers to regenerate it.

If you've made it this far, give yourself a hug. There's good news coming up, so let's power on.

This dependence on chemicals can (and must!) be turned around. Farmers all over the world, seeing their soil die before their eyes, are looking for sustainable alternatives, and regenerative agriculture is providing a way to grow food that nourishes rather than depletes the soil.

By observing the way the natural world worked, people like Allan Savory have used their learnings to create some key guiding principles of regen' farming. Keep reading for these principles in a nutshell.

1. Avoid tilling

Healthy, rich soil should look porous – a bit like a sponge. Tilling the soil breaks up all that spongy organic matter, releasing the carbon that is stored in it.

2. Increase biodiversity

Nature is diverse. In an untouched, natural environment, rarely will you see only one type of grass, crop or animal. Rather, it's a cacophony of animal and plant species all working together. The regen' farmer will want to increase biodiversity on the land, and avoid mono-cropping or the dominance of one crop.

3. Practise cell grazing

This is a type of grazing that allows livestock to move around and prevents overgrazing of any one paddock. Regen' farmers will often create 'cell' paddocks by dividing larger paddocks into many smaller ones and will move their stock between them once or twice a day.

4. Plant cover crops

One of the worst things for soil is to leave it bare. Cover crops do for the soil what clothes do for our skin, protecting it from sun and wind damage, but also helping to keep it moist. The roots penetrate the soil, keeping it porous and permeable, allowing water to make its way down. Cover crops also contribute nutrients and attract beneficial pollinators.

5. Little to no chemical inputs

I'm not sure I have to explain this one; I think you get the point. But there isn't a total ban on chemicals. There may be a good reason that a regen' farmer needs to use chemical intervention. If buffalo flies are driving the cows mad, a chemical repellent may be used to help mitigate the herd's distress. Mick Green, who started the regen' process on our farm along with Mum, says that chemicals are 'a tool in my back pocket that I use only after exhausting every other natural solution'. Knowing the destruction they cause, a regen' farmer would certainly be limiting chemical inputs, and many wouldn't use them at all.

It's not easy to transition from conventional farming to regen', but it is possible. It takes incentive, commitment, investment and a lot of 'unlearning'. Farmers all over the world have taken these principles and applied them to the way they farm. Some might only apply one or two, others use them all simultaneously – different things work for different farmers. But the overall objective is the same: to improve the ecology of the land and soil, and, as Mick says, to 'leave the land better than how we found it'. Who can argue with that?

Our farm started the conversion from conventional farming to regen' practices in 2019, and it's now a proudly working regen' farm. You can learn more about how this process worked in Mum's film, *Rachel's Farm* (see page 198). Our food business sources meat exclusively from regen' farms, as we believe that selecting growers and producers who prioritise soil health will help us move towards a healthier future.

mornings

Creamy Mango-Nut Breakfast Trifle

This is a delight to eat on a summer's morning while enjoying the sunrise. If your mangoes aren't quite ripe when you buy them, don't despair; mangoes continue to ripen after being picked. Try placing them in a paper bag to help speed up the process.

SERVES 2

1 cup (260 g) Greek-style
    yoghurt, or coconut yoghurt
1–2 tablespoons honey
½ teaspoon vanilla extract
¼ cup (20 g) shredded coconut
¼ cup (40 g) macadamia nuts,
    roughly chopped
1 large ripe mango, peeled,
    stone removed, diced
½ cup (45 g) Granola (page 38)

In a bowl, mix the yoghurt with 1 tablespoon of the honey and the vanilla extract. Stir until smooth and well combined, then set aside.

In a small dry frying pan, toast the shredded coconut over medium heat until lightly golden and aromatic. Remove from the heat and leave to cool.

Combine the macadamia nuts and toasted coconut in a bowl.

To assemble each trifle, start with a spoonful of the macadamia and coconut mix in the bottom of each serving glass or bowl. Top with a thick layer of the creamy yoghurt mixture, followed by a layer of diced mango.

Add another layer of creamy yoghurt mixture, some more mango, then finish the trifle with a generous sprinkling of granola for a delightful crunch.

Drizzle the remaining honey over the top for an extra touch of sweetness.

Granola with Banana Peanut Butter Mash

The only problem with this granola is once you start eating it, it's almost impossible to stop. Trust me, I make several large batches a week and have to have a serious word with myself to make sure it stays the course! Allow the granola to cool completely before transferring to a jar or tub, otherwise it'll sweat and lose its crunch.

SERVES 1

1 banana, peeled
1 tablespoon peanut butter
4 tablespoons Granola
  (see below)
2 tablespoons Greek-style or
  plain yoghurt (optional)

MAKES 12 SERVES

GRANOLA
¼ cup (55 g) coconut oil
2 tablespoons hemp oil
  (optional)
¼ cup (90 g) honey
¼ cup (45 g) coconut sugar
1 teaspoon ground cinnamon
1 teaspoon ground allspice
½ cup (85 g) hemp seeds
½ cup (75 g) macadamia nuts,
  roughly chopped
½ cup (65 g) slivered almonds,
  roughly chopped
½ cup (50 g) pecans,
  roughly chopped
¼ cup (40 g) pepitas
  (pumpkin seeds)
2 cups (130 g) shredded
  coconut

Preheat the oven to 150°C (300°F). Line a large baking tray with baking paper.

To make the granola, combine all the ingredients except the shredded coconut in a large mixing bowl.

Spread the granola mix on the baking tray in one even layer. Bake for 30 minutes.

Halfway through the cooking time, remove from the oven, add the coconut and mix well, then return and continue baking for another 15 minutes.

When the coconut is just lightly toasted, remove from the oven and leave to cool.

In a mixing bowl, roughly mash the banana with a fork. Add the peanut butter and mash again.

Transfer to a serving bowl and sprinkle the toasted granola on top. Dollop with yoghurt, if using, or simply enjoy as it is.

Any extra granola will keep in an airtight container for up to 6 months.

Creamy Coconut Quinoa Porridge with Mixed Berries

This is creamy and warming, with a hint of tartness from the berries and a surprisingly moreish texture from the quinoa. Just remember to rinse and drain your quinoa a few times before cooking it to remove the saponins coating the grains, which can irritate the stomach.

SERVES 2

1 cup (200 g) quinoa, rinsed
   and drained
400 ml (14 fl oz) tin coconut
   milk
½ teaspoon ground cinnamon
½ teaspoon ground nutmeg
a pinch of salt
2 tablespoons honey
1½ cups (195 g) mixed berries,
   thawed if frozen
1 tablespoon coconut sugar
1 tablespoon lemon juice

Add the quinoa to a saucepan with the coconut milk, spices and salt. Bring to a gentle boil over medium heat.

Reduce the heat to low, cover with a lid and simmer for 15–20 minutes, or until the quinoa is tender and has absorbed most of the liquid. Fluff up with a fork and mix in the honey.

Meanwhile, throw the berries, sugar and lemon juice in a blender and blitz until combined (some bigger bits are fine).

Serve the quinoa porridge with the blitzed mixed berries on top.

Winter Apple Cinnamon Porridge

Get ready to cosy up with this porridge – because who needs a winter coat when you can have a bowl of this deliciousness to warm you up? The classic pairing of apple and cinnamon is truly like snuggling into your favourite jumper.

SERVES 2

1 cup (95 g) rolled oats
2 cups (500 ml) full-cream milk, or coconut milk
½ teaspoon ground cinnamon
¼ teaspoon ground nutmeg
a pinch of salt
2 tablespoons honey, or maple syrup
2 tablespoons butter
1 large apple, cored and diced
½ cup (50 g) pecans, almonds or walnuts, roughly chopped
zest of 1 small orange

In a saucepan, combine the rolled oats, milk, cinnamon, nutmeg and salt. Bring the mixture to a gentle boil over medium heat.

Reduce the heat to low and simmer the oats, stirring occasionally, until creamy and tender. This should take about 5–7 minutes.

Remove from the heat and stir the honey into the porridge to sweeten. Adjust the sweetness to your liking.

In a small frying pan, melt the butter over medium heat.

Add the apple and sauté for 3–4 minutes, or until softened and lightly caramelised. Stir the sautéed apples into the cooked porridge.

Toast the chopped nuts in the same frying pan for a couple of minutes over low heat until fragrant and lightly browned. Remove from the heat.

Serve the porridge in bowls and top with the toasted nuts and some orange zest.

Banana Scramble Pancake

This is, hands down, Zan's favourite breakfast meal. It was once a favourite with Tashi too when he was little, but he opts for more adult sophistication these days. In my opinion it's a great breakfast whatever your age. Hover at the stove for this one though, because there is an ideal time to flip: too early and it'll be a mess, too late and you'll dry out the whole pancake.

SERVES 1

1 ripe banana, peeled and mashed (the riper the sweeter)
2 tablespoons shredded coconut
2 teaspoons salted butter
2 eggs, beaten
¼ teaspoon ground cinnamon (optional)
1 tablespoon coconut oil
1 teaspoon honey, or to taste
Greek-style yoghurt and blueberries, to serve

In a large mixing bowl, combine the banana, shredded coconut, butter, eggs and cinnamon, if using.

Heat the coconut oil in a non-stick frying pan over medium heat.

Once hot, add the banana mixture to the pan and gently tilt it so that the mixture spreads out evenly over the whole base of the pan. Cook for at least 2 minutes before checking to see if the underside is nice and brown.

Once browned, either flip the pancake over with a flick of the pan (if you're feeling brave) or use a spatula to turn it and cook until browned on the other side, about another 2 minutes.

Immediately remove the pan from the heat to avoid overcooking (nobody wants a dry banana pancake!).

Flip onto a plate and drizzle with a little (or a lot) of honey before serving with yoghurt and blueberries.

Corn and Chilli

How good does this one look? And it's even better to taste: vibrant and full of freshness, but with a spicy kick. Think of it as a corn version of shakshuka but just as flavourful and easy to make.

SERVES 2

2 ears of corn, outer leaves removed, trimmed
2 tablespoons olive oil
1 small brown onion, finely chopped
2 garlic cloves, minced
½ teaspoon dried oregano
½ teaspoon chipotle powder
1–2 long red chillies, destemmed and finely chopped
1 red capsicum (pepper), destemmed, cored and diced
1 green capsicum (pepper), destemmed, cored and diced
4 eggs
½ –1 avocado, sliced, to serve
juice of ½ lime, to serve
¼ bunch coriander (cilantro), leaves left whole or roughly chopped, to serve

Preheat the oven to 160°C (315°F).

Bring a large saucepan of salted water to the boil. Place the corn cobs in the water and bring back to the boil, then reduce the heat to medium and simmer strongly for 3–5 minutes before removing from the heat. Drain and, once the corn has cooled a little, cut the kernels off and set aside.

Heat the oil in a large ovenproof frying pan over medium heat. Add the onion and garlic and sauté for 3–4 minutes.

Add the oregano, chipotle powder, chilli and capsicum to the frying pan and stir. Cook for another 5–6 minutes before adding the corn kernels.

Create four depressions in the mixture with the back of a spoon and crack an egg into each one.

Transfer the pan to the oven and cook for 8–10 minutes, or until the eggs are cooked to your liking.

Remove from the oven, season to taste with salt and pepper, and serve with avocado and a squeeze of lime juice. Scatter the chopped coriander on top.

Pan-fried Chicken Livers on Toast

When I first met Til she was vegetarian, having been vegan for years, so the fact that this is now, hands down, her favourite breakfast is testimony to her openness to a new approach to eating. I'm a big fan too. And, given livers are densely nutritious, you can start the day knowing you've already put some goodness in your body.

SERVES 2

3 tablespoons extra-virgin
   olive oil
2 eschalots, or 1 small brown
   onion, thinly sliced
2 garlic cloves, sliced
¼ teaspoon chilli flakes
5 thyme sprigs
1 tablespoon fresh oregano
   leaves
300 g (10½ oz) chicken livers,
   trimmed and roughly
   chopped into 1 cm (½ inch)
   pieces
1½ cups (70 g) baby English
   spinach leaves
1 teaspoon salted butter, plus
   extra for buttering toast
2 slices of gluten-free
   or sourdough bread
juice of ½ lemon, plus wedges
   to serve

Heat the olive oil in a frying pan over medium heat. Add the eschalot, garlic and chilli and sauté for 5 minutes.

Increase the heat to high, add the thyme, oregano and chicken livers and cook until the livers brown, about 8 minutes. Once browned, stir in the baby spinach.

Add the butter and continue cooking for another 2–3 minutes, or until the spinach has wilted.

Meanwhile, pop the bread into the toaster.

Remove the livers from the heat, drizzle the lemon juice on top and season with salt and pepper to taste.

Generously butter the toast, top with the chicken livers and serve.

Bubble and Squeak Omelette

Perhaps I'm revealing my British heritage in this dish, but bubble and squeak is synonymous with a good ol' English breakfast, and it's a great way of using ageing greens, or last night's leftovers. Take your time while cooking it to ensure the bottom of the omelette becomes nice and caramelised, which adds a secondary layer of flavour to this dish.

SERVES 4

1 tablespoon extra-virgin
    olive oil
2 tablespoons salted butter
1 brown onion, sliced
2 eschalots, chopped
200 g (7 oz) greens (broccoli,
    cabbage, brussels sprouts,
    spinach – anything that
    needs using up), chopped
400 g (14 oz) leftover roasted
    potatoes, or mashed potato
4–6 eggs, beaten

Heat the oil and 1 tablespoon of the butter in a large ovenproof frying pan over medium heat. Add the onion and eschalot and sauté for 6 minutes, or until softened.

Add the greens and cook for another 6 minutes or so until they begin to soften, then remove from the pan and set aside.

Preheat the oven to 180°C (350°F).

Heat the remaining butter in the pan over medium heat, then add the potato and season with salt and pepper. Press down to ensure the potato becomes lovely and golden.

Spread the greens over the top, then add the eggs and cook over low heat until the egg is just set, about 6 minutes. Use a spatula to loosen the omelette from the base of the pan.

Transfer the pan to the oven and cook the omelette for another 5–8 minutes until lightly golden and fully set.

Spicy Green Brekkie Bowl

Rise and shine, spice enthusiasts! Say goodbye to bland breakfasts (life is too short) and hello to this brekkie bowl – the morning kick your tastebuds never knew they needed.

SERVES 2

SPICY DRESSING

2 tablespoons Greek-style or plain yoghurt

1 tablespoon Chilli Sauce (page 194), or sriracha

1 tablespoon lime juice

1 teaspoon honey

BOWL

½ cup (65 g) frozen peas

1 cup (60 g) broccoli florets

1 cup (50 g) baby English spinach leaves

1 cup (35 g) rocket (arugula)

100 g (3½ oz) cherry tomatoes, halved or quartered

4 eggs

2 tablespoons pepitas (pumpkin seeds), to serve

1 avocado, halved, to serve

lime juice, to serve

Combine all the ingredients for the dressing in a bowl, season to taste with salt and pepper, and set aside.

Bring a saucepan of salted water to the boil and cook the peas and broccoli together for 3–4 minutes, then drain and set aside until cool.

In a large mixing bowl, gently toss the spinach, rocket and cherry tomatoes with the peas and broccoli. Drizzle the dressing on top and toss again. Check and adjust the seasoning.

Either poach or fry the eggs – whichever you prefer.

Transfer the salad to a serving bowl, sprinkle the pepitas on top and serve with the avocado halves and eggs. Finish with a squeeze of lime juice and a little more seasoning.

Our Kedgeree

Rather than the traditional rice-based kedgeree, we opt for a lighter version using cauliflower rice. Kedgeree can easily be (and is traditionally) a breakfast dish, but given it takes a little more prep, it's doubtful you'll be rustling it up before the kids head out for school. Save it for a lazy weekend brunch instead. Ideally select Marine Stewardship Council (MSC)–certified mackerel or a similar smoked fish. This will ensure you're supporting a fishery that abides by quotas to promote sustainable fish stocks.

SERVES 4

2 tablespoons ghee, or
coconut oil
1 brown onion, finely chopped
2 garlic cloves, minced
2 cm (¾ inch) piece ginger,
peeled and grated
1 teaspoon ground cumin
1 teaspoon ground coriander
1 teaspoon ground turmeric
¼ teaspoon cayenne pepper
1 head cauliflower, florets grated
or pulsed in a food processor
to a rice-like texture
400 g (14 oz) cooked smoked
fish (ideally mackerel), flaked
¾ cup (100 g) frozen peas,
thawed
¼ bunch parsley, roughly
chopped
¼ bunch coriander (cilantro),
roughly chopped
juice of 1 lemon
4 soft-boiled eggs, peeled and
halved or quartered, to serve

Heat the ghee in a large frying pan over medium heat. Add the onion and sauté for 4–5 minutes before adding the garlic and ginger and cooking for a further 2–3 minutes.

Add the spices and stir well to coat the onion.

Add the cauliflower rice to the pan, mixing until thoroughly coated in the spiced ghee. Cook for 5–6 minutes, or until the cauliflower is tender but not mushy.

Fold in the flaked fish and peas, allowing them to heat through with the cauliflower rice, then remove from the heat.

Mix in the parsley and coriander, and squeeze in the lemon juice. Season, then gently combine. Serve with the eggs.

66 Food can bring comfort and communion. It holds the power to regenerate our ecosystems and our health.

Chilli Con Carne and Guacamole on Toast

Chilli con carne is a delicious dish and one I've loved my entire life. We make it for The Good Farm Shop, and I eat it every morning for a late breakfast. It might not be everyone's cup of tea, but I find it the perfect way to start my day. I've upped the breakfast ante here by first spreading the bread with chilli con carne, then dolloping on guacamole. It's always a good decision.

SERVES 4

GUACAMOLE
3 ripe avocados, peeled,
   stones removed
½ red onion, finely chopped
1 jalapeño chilli, destemmed,
   deseeded and finely chopped
¼ bunch coriander (cilantro),
   finely chopped
juice of 2 limes, zest of 1 lime
1 teaspoon ground cumin
½ teaspoon smoked paprika

CHILLI CON CARNE
2 tablespoons extra-virgin
   olive oil
2 small brown onions,
   finely chopped
4 garlic cloves, minced
2 tablespoons dried oregano
2 tablespoons ground cumin
2 teaspoons sweet paprika
2 teaspoons smoked paprika
1–2 teaspoons chilli powder
1 tablespoon tomato paste
   (concentrated purée)
500 g (1 lb 2 oz) minced
   (ground) beef, at room
   temperature
600 g (1 lb 5 oz) tinned diced
   tomatoes
400 g (14 oz) tin kidney beans,
   drained and rinsed
4 slices gluten-free
   or sourdough bread

Begin by combining all the ingredients for the guacamole in a mixing bowl, mashing the avocado with a fork until combined but with some rustic texture. Place a piece of plastic wrap directly on the surface of the guacamole and refrigerate until needed.

For the chilli con carne, heat the oil in a large frying pan over medium heat and add the onion and garlic. Sauté for 5–6 minutes before adding the oregano and spices, then continue cooking for another 5 minutes. Add the tomato paste and stir for 1–2 minutes.

Increase the heat to high and add the beef. Stir for several minutes until the meat is nicely browned.

Reduce the heat to medium and add the tinned tomatoes. Mix well, and cook for 10 minutes.

Add the kidney beans and cook for another 15 minutes over medium–low heat. Season to taste, then remove from the heat.

Pop the bread in the toaster or grill until lightly toasted. Slather the toast with the chilli con carne and add a generous dollop of guacamole. Season with salt and pepper, then serve.

Green Salsa Eggs

As a family, we've made our Salsa Verde (page 188) about a million times (mild exaggeration, but not far off) and discovered you can add it to almost any dish and it will just work ... eggs being no exception!

SERVES 2

1 tablespoon salted butter
4–5 large eggs, lightly beaten
2–3 tablespoons Salsa Verde
   (page 188)

For the eggs, heat the butter in a frying pan over medium heat. Once it has melted and coated the bottom of the pan, give the eggs a season and add them to the pan. Cook for 3–4 minutes, gently folding the eggs with a wooden spoon or spatula.

Once the eggs start to firm up, add the salsa verde and fold it through the eggs. Continue to cook until the eggs are cooked to your liking (keep in mind that they will continue cooking once they're out of the pan).

Transfer to a plate, season with salt and a little black pepper and enjoy.

Shakshuka

Our shakshuka is one of our bestsellers at The Good Farm Shop, and for good reason: it is the hero of any weekend brunch spread and lasts a while in the fridge. It's also quick to whip together.

SERVES 3–4

3 tablespoons extra-virgin
   olive oil
2 brown onions, roughly
   chopped
6 garlic cloves, roughly
   chopped
1½ tablespoons ground cumin
1 teaspoon sweet paprika
2 teaspoons smoked paprika
1 teaspoon sumac
½–1 teaspoon cayenne pepper
3 kg (6 lb 12 oz) roma tomatoes,
   cored and roughly chopped
4 eggs
chopped parsley, to serve

Heat the oil in a saucepan over medium heat and sauté the onion and garlic for 5 minutes, stirring occasionally, before adding the spices. Stir through.

Cook for a further 15 minutes, ensuring the spices don't catch on the bottom of the pan. Add a little more oil if necessary.

Add the chopped tomatoes and mix well, then reduce the heat to medium–low and cook for 30 minutes, stirring occasionally.

Season to taste with salt and pepper, then either blitz the tomatoes with a stick blender, or transfer the mixture to a blender and blitz. Set aside 300 ml (10½ fl oz) of the sauce for the shakshuka. The rest can be stored in an airtight container in the fridge for up to 10 days.

Add the sauce to a small frying pan.

Make four depressions with the back of a spoon and crack an egg into each depression. Place the pan over medium heat and cook the eggs for 8 minutes in the sauce, or until cooked to your liking. (You could also cook them in the oven instead – bake at 160°C/315°F for 6 minutes, or until cooked to your liking.) Sprinkle some chopped parsley on top and serve.

afternoons

Chunky Heirloom Tomato Salad with Crispy Bacon and Anchovies

This has to be one of my favourite salads of all time: the sweetness from the juicy tomatoes against the crispy saltiness of the bacon. Heaven! And don't listen to the anchovy naysayers either – these little fish bring all the umami here, and they're a tomato's best friend. If you really want to, you could use capers instead.

SERVES 4

4 asparagus spears, ends trimmed, halved
1 teaspoon extra-virgin olive oil
6 rashers streaky bacon
4–6 large heirloom tomatoes, cored and thickly sliced or roughly chopped into large chunks
6–8 anchovy fillets
4–6 tablespoons Tangy Lime Dressing (page 192)
50 g (1¾ oz) goat's feta, to serve
80 g (2¾ oz) rocket (arugula), to serve

Bring a saucepan of salted water to the boil, drop in the asparagus and boil for 2 minutes before draining and running under cool water. Set aside.

Heat the olive oil in a frying pan over medium–high heat. Once hot, add the bacon rashers and cook until crispy, about 2–3 minutes on each side. Remove from the heat and set aside.

Put the tomatoes, anchovy fillets and asparagus in a large mixing bowl and lightly toss. Now dress the salad with the tangy dressing and toss again. Transfer to a serving bowl.

'Smash' the crispy bacon using a knife and sprinkle it over the salad.

Top with the crumbled feta and rocket, and season to taste (just bear in mind that the anchovies, feta and bacon are already salty).

Pan-fried Mushrooms with Thyme and Lemon on Toast

My parents owned a pub in the UK, which meant that growing up I had constant access to the kitchen. One of my favourite things to make was mushrooms on toast. Back then, it was button mushrooms microwaved in butter, possibly finished with lemon, then dumped on a slice of Sunblest white bread. Gone is the cheap bread and the microwave, but my love for this dish remains. When adding lemon juice, it's generally better to do it at the end to avoid the dish becoming a little acrid on the palate.

SERVES 2

2 tablespoons extra-virgin olive oil
3–4 thyme sprigs
1 teaspoon chopped rosemary leaves
2 garlic cloves, minced
2 handfuls of mushrooms (button, King brown, portobello), halved or left whole if small
2 tablespoons salted butter, plus extra for buttering the toast
2 slices of gluten-free or sourdough bread
juice of ½ lemon
¼ cup (35 g) feta, to serve

Heat 1 tablespoon of the olive oil in a large frying pan over medium heat before adding the herbs and garlic. Cook for 2–3 minutes.

Add the mushrooms and mix well with the garlic and herbs. Add the remaining olive oil and butter and cook for 8–10 minutes, or until the mushrooms are softened and cooked through.

Pop the bread in the toaster.

Remove the mushrooms from the heat and drizzle with lemon juice. Season with salt and pepper.

Butter the toast, then pile your mushrooms on top and crumble on the feta to finish.

Cheesy Ragu Jacket Potato

The Cheesy Ragu Jacket Potato is the comfort food champion of your dreams: a perfectly baked potato, golden and crisp on the outside, fluffy on the inside, generously stuffed with our popular ragu and plenty of golden cheese.

SERVES 4

4 sweet potatoes
2 tablespoons extra-virgin olive oil
1 large brown onion, chopped
1 tablespoon dried oregano
1 tablespoon dried basil
¼ cup (60 g) tomato paste (concentrated purée)
500 g (1 lb 2 oz) minced (ground) beef
2 × 400 g (14 oz) tins diced tomatoes
2 tablespoons salted butter
200 g (7 oz) grated cheddar

Preheat the oven to 190°C (375°F).

Place the potatoes on a baking tray and season with salt and pepper. Bake for 40 minutes, or until the potatoes soften.

While the potatoes cook, heat the olive oil in a large frying pan over medium–high heat and sauté the onion for 5–6 minutes. Add the herbs and stir.

Add the tomato paste, stir and cook for a further 2–3 minutes, then add the beef and increase the heat slightly to brown the mince.

Once browned, add the tinned tomatoes and stir through. Return the heat to medium and cook for another 25 minutes. Season the ragu to taste and remove from the heat.

Once the potatoes are cooked, remove from the oven. Cut a slit lengthways in each potato about three-quarters of the way through and open it out to create a pocket. Add a small dollop of butter inside each before topping with a generous serve of bolognese (it doesn't have to be neat). Finish with the grated cheese.

Baked Salmon with Orange, Dill and Pistachio Kernels

We were fortunate to host the incredible Dr Zach Bush – microbiome and food systems expert – for a lunch, and this was something I rustled up for him and our other guests. It was daunting cooking for someone I respect so highly, but the food was a hit, as was meeting him in the flesh.

When buying seafood, always look out for the MSC (Marine Stewardship Council) certification (a blue tick on the label). MSC is the highest standard of sustainable seafood in the world, and fisheries have to adhere to rigid guidelines to be awarded accreditation and maintain it. It is the fisheries, not the fish species itself, that receive this sustainability accreditation, which promotes sustainable fishing practices by enforcing quotas that ensure healthy fish stocks and minimise by-catch.

Buying from a MSC-certified producer is the closest equivalent to buying from a holistically managed farm. The fishmonger *should* know if they are selling MSC, but I would encourage you to do some investigating of your own when buying fish (just as you would when buying meat, chicken, eggs and vegetables) to ensure you can shop with confidence.

SERVES 12–14

1.5 kg (3 lb 5 oz) salmon
  fillet, pin-boned, at room
  temperature
2 tablespoons extra-virgin
  olive oil
½ cup (70 g) pistachio kernels,
  crushed
¼ cup (15 g) finely chopped dill

DRESSING
juice of 4 large oranges
1 teaspoon wholegrain mustard
1 teaspoon honey
⅓ cup (20 g) chopped dill
⅓ cup (20 g) chopped parsley
100 ml (3½ fl oz) olive oil
1 teaspoon sumac

Preheat the oven to 180°C (350°F). Line a large baking tray with baking paper or foil.

Place the salmon on the tray, skin side down. Drizzle the oil over the top and season with salt and pepper. Roast in the oven for 25–30 minutes (depending on thickness), or until the core temperature reaches 55°C (130°F).

Meanwhile, put the dressing ingredients in a blender and blitz until combined, then season to taste with salt and pepper.

Combine the pistachio and dill in a small bowl.

Once cooked, remove the fish from the oven and allow to rest for 5 minutes.

To serve, pour the dressing over the fish, then scatter the pistachio and dill mixture on top.

" It is everyone's
responsibility to question
the provenance of the food
they put in their basket.

Paleo Veggie Slice

This is a great recipe for using any ageing veggies, and was inspired by a paleo bread I had at a much-loved Bondi cafe (sadly not there any longer), which had a great menu. It was also where I first met Til. She paid me zero attention as we were introduced. I was rocked by her beauty. The egg in this recipe is the binder and the bicarbonate of soda (baking soda) gives it a little air so it's not so dense, but if you don't have any in the cupboard, it's no stress.

SERVES 4

4 large carrots, grated
6 zucchini (courgettes), grated
½ cup (95 g) pitted kalamata
olives, roughly chopped
¼ cup (55 g) semi-dried
tomatoes, drained and
roughly chopped
2 teaspoons dried oregano
1 teaspoon dried thyme
10–12 eggs, lightly whisked
1 teaspoon bicarbonate of soda
(baking soda)
50 g (1¾ oz) salted butter, plus
extra for greasing

Preheat the oven to 160°C (315°F).

In a large mixing bowl, combine all the ingredients and lightly whisk for 30 seconds. Season, mix again, and set aside.

Grease a 23 × 33 cm (9 × 13 in) baking dish with a little butter and pour in the egg and veggie mixture.

Bake in the oven for 30–40 minutes, or until golden brown. Remove from the oven and serve.

Chargrilled Zucchini Salad

I happened upon this recipe when our little veggie patch began to sprout zucchini (courgettes) in prolific proportions. This salad was number 56 in the 235 ways to eat zucchini that summer.

SERVES 2

⅓ cup (80 ml) extra-virgin olive oil, plus extra for brushing
4 garlic cloves, chopped
2 celery stalks, trimmed and chopped
½ bunch parsley, leaves roughly chopped, stalks finely chopped
1 teaspoon chilli flakes
1 tablespoon capers, drained and rinsed
6 anchovy fillets
1 tablespoon red wine vinegar
3 large zucchini (courgettes), trimmed and halved lengthways
50 g (1¾ oz) pistachio kernels
1 teaspoon lemon zest

Heat the olive oil in a small frying pan over low heat.

Add the garlic, celery, parsley stalks, chilli flakes, capers, anchovy fillets and vinegar and cook gently for 15 minutes. Remove from the heat and transfer to a mixing bowl. Set aside.

Heat a chargrill pan over high heat.

Brush both sides of the zucchini with a little olive oil, then place in the pan and cook for 3–4 minutes on each side, or until nicely charred.

Once charred, remove from the heat and allow to cool before cutting into small wedges.

Add to the celery mix along with the parsley leaves, pistachio kernels and lemon zest, and gently mix to combine. Season to taste and serve.

Epic Salad Sandwiches with Fried Egg

When I arrived in Sydney as a young lad, sandwich bars were the go-to places for lunch, but sadly they have been replaced over the years by trendier cafes. Just a part of the culinary evolution, I guess. I used to enjoy the novelty of choosing the ingredients, so feel free to add your favourites – anything goes.

SERVES 2

1 tablespoon extra-virgin olive oil
2–4 eggs
4 slices of gluten-free or sourdough bread
2 tablespoons salted butter
4–6 lettuce leaves, such as romaine, iceberg or butter
1 large ripe tomato, thinly sliced
¼ red onion, thinly sliced
1 carrot, grated
2 tablespoons sauerkraut
½ avocado, sliced

HERB MAYONNAISE
¼ cup (60 g) mayonnaise
2 tablespoons Greek-style or plain yoghurt
juice of ¼ lemon
¼ cup (15 g) basil leaves
¼ cup (5 g) parsley leaves
1 garlic clove, peeled
1 teaspoon capers, drained and rinsed

Begin by blitzing all the ingredients for the herb mayonnaise in a blender or food processor until combined. Season to taste with salt and pepper and set aside.

Heat the olive oil in a frying pan over medium heat. Crack in the eggs and cook for 3–5 minutes, or until cooked to your liking. Remove from the heat and set aside.

Begin building the sandwiches by spreading the bread with a good layer of butter, followed by a slather of the herb mayo.

Next, add the lettuce, tomato, onion, carrot, sauerkraut and avocado. Lay one or two eggs on top and make a small incision in the yolk to allow it to run through the sandwich.

Season and get messy.

Hummus with Roasted Veggies

I love this dish for its rich flavours and colours. Hummus has been made for centuries, with an early iteration of the dish recorded in a thirteenth-century Arabic cookbook. Sure, you can buy a shop-bought version, but it's way more satisfying to whip up your own, and it takes very little time. Plus, chickpeas are a good source of fibre and plant protein, so making it yourself is a no-brainer. As a rule of thumb, veggies cook best at a high heat, otherwise they 'stew' and lose a lot of moisture. You're looking for plenty of caramelisation too, which adds to the colour and taste.

SERVES 4

2 beetroots (beets), trimmed, peeled and cut into bite-sized chunks
2 tablespoons extra-virgin olive oil
2 teaspoons za'atar
2 red onions, peeled and quartered
2 baby fennel bulbs, trimmed and quartered
¼ cup (15 g) chopped dill
50 g (1¾ oz) goat's feta (see Note)

HUMMUS
400 g (14 oz) tin chickpeas, drained and rinsed
⅓ cup (90 g) tahini
2 garlic cloves, peeled
juice of 1 lemon
1 teaspoon ground cumin
1 teaspoon za'atar
1 tablespoon olive oil

Preheat the oven to 160°C (315°F).

Place the beetroot and olive oil in a roasting tin and toss together to coat the beetroot in oil. Season with salt and pepper and roast in the oven for 40 minutes.

Remove from the oven and add the za'atar, onion and fennel. Toss lightly to coat the veggies in the oil and spices. Return to the oven and increase the heat to 180°C (350°F). Roast for another 35 minutes, or until the veggies are golden and cooked through.

Meanwhile, place all the ingredients for the hummus in a blender or food processor with ½ cup (125 ml) water and blitz until smooth. Transfer to a bowl.

Remove the veggies from the oven and season to taste with salt and pepper.

Dress a serving plate with the hummus and serve with the veggies, sprinkling both with dill, and feta on the side.

Note

You can replace the goat's feta with halloumi, if you wish.

Curried Egg Lettuce Cigars

Curried eggs were a real thing when I was a kid, but they've since been relegated to the kitsch and unfashionable food of the seventies, a time when buffet-style gatherings and potlucks reigned. However, I'm a believer the curried egg will enjoy the renaissance it deserves, starting here. Feel free to don a pair of flares and a turtleneck while you prepare these.

SERVES 2-4

6 hard-boiled eggs, peeled and chopped or mashed with a fork
2 tablespoons Lemon Mayonnaise (page 191), plus extra if needed
1 teaspoon curry powder
½ teaspoon ground cumin
¼ teaspoon ground turmeric
2 eschalots, trimmed and finely sliced
¼ cup (15 g) finely chopped dill
8–10 large butter lettuce leaves, or lettuce of your choice

DIPPING SAUCE
¼ cup (70 g) Greek-style yoghurt, or sour cream
juice of ½ lemon
1 teaspoon honey
1 tablespoon chopped coriander (cilantro)
1 tablespoon chopped mint

In a mixing bowl, combine the egg, mayonnaise, curry powder, cumin and turmeric. Season to taste with salt and pepper. Gently mix the ingredients until well combined and the curried egg filling is creamy (add more mayonnaise if necessary).

Next, add the eschalot and dill and mix again, then season to taste.

Mix all the ingredients for the dipping sauce in a bowl, season to taste and set aside.

Lay a lettuce leaf on a chopping board. Place a generous dollop of the egg mixture on the lettuce leaf along the edge nearest to you, leaving some room on the sides to fold.

Grab the edge of the lettuce nearest you and fold it over the egg mixture, then neatly fold in the sides. Continue rolling to create a cigar shape, then place on a serving plate with the folded leaf edge facing down.

Serve the rolled lettuce cigars with the dipping sauce.

Caesar Salad with Roasted Chickpeas and Creamy Avocado Dressing

Caesar salad may have withstood the test of time, but croutons are most definitely out, and golden chickpeas are in! This isn't your average leafy affair – it's a crunchy, creamy and downright delicious experience. A salad for all seasons!

SERVES 4

400 g (14 oz) tin chickpeas, drained and rinsed
1 tablespoon extra-virgin olive oil
1 teaspoon garlic powder
½ teaspoon paprika
½ teaspoon ground cumin
1 head romaine lettuce, trimmed
½ cup (70 g) cherry tomatoes, halved
1 small red onion, sliced
2 ripe avocados, stones removed, sliced
6–8 slices crispy bacon, crumbled
½ cup (50 g) grated parmesan cheese, to serve

DRESSING
1 ripe avocado
2 tablespoons coconut cream, or Greek-style yoghurt
juice of ½ lemon
¼ cup (60 ml) extra-virgin olive oil
1 garlic clove, minced
1 teaspoon dijon mustard

Preheat the oven to 200°C (400°F). Line a baking tray with baking paper.

Pat the chickpeas dry with paper towel to remove excess moisture.

In a bowl, toss the dried chickpeas with the olive oil, garlic powder, paprika, cumin and some salt and pepper until they are evenly coated.

Spread the seasoned chickpeas in a single layer on the baking tray. Roast in the oven for 20–25 minutes, or until the chickpeas are crispy and golden brown. Shake the tray gently halfway through cooking to ensure the chickpeas crisp evenly. Remove from the oven and set aside.

In a large salad bowl, combine the lettuce, tomato, onion, avocado and bacon.

For the dressing, combine all the ingredients in a blender or food processor and blitz until smooth and creamy.

Drizzle the creamy avocado dressing over the salad and gently toss to evenly coat the ingredients, or spoon some dressing onto a serving plate and arrange the salad on top. Sprinkle the roasted chickpeas and parmesan on top, season to taste with salt and pepper, and serve.

Fiery Veggie Stir-fry

This dish has it all – except the meat or seafood. But what it lacks in protein it more than makes up for in colour, freshness, nutrients and flavour.

SERVES 4

2 tablespoons coconut oil
1 red onion, thinly sliced
4 garlic cloves, minced
2 cm (¾ inch) piece ginger,
    peeled and minced
1 red capsicum (pepper),
    destemmed, cored and
    thinly sliced
1 yellow capsicum (pepper),
    destemmed, cored and
    thinly sliced
2 cups (120 g) broccoli florets
100 g (3½ oz) sugar-snap peas,
    trimmed
1 carrot, thinly sliced
1 cup (200 g) corn kernels
2 portobello mushrooms, sliced
1 tablespoon sesame seeds,
    to serve
¼ bunch coriander (cilantro),
    roughly chopped, to serve

SAUCE
3 tablespoons tamari
2 tablespoons Chilli Sauce
    (page 194), or sriracha or
    sambal oelek
1 tablespoon honey
1 tablespoon rice vinegar
1 teaspoon sesame oil

In a small mixing bowl, whisk together the sauce ingredients and set to one side.

Heat the coconut oil in a large frying pan or wok over medium heat.

Add the onion and stir-fry for 3–4 minutes until it begins to caramelise. Throw in the garlic and ginger and stir-fry for 1–2 minutes.

Add the remaining veggies and cook until tender, about 6–7 minutes.

Pour in the sauce you made earlier and cook for 2–3 minutes, tossing often.

Remove from the heat and sprinkle some sesame seeds and coriander on top to finish.

Curry Butter Swordfish with Beans

As you've probably noticed by now, I'm a fan of butter ... it makes my world go round. I often use it to hold and carry the flavours of herbs, garlic and spices. Here, I've packed the butter with my favourite fragrant spices – it's basically a shortcut to a delicious curry.

SERVES 2

2 Marine Stewardship Council–
    certified swordfish steaks
1 teaspoon coconut oil
80 g (2¾ oz) green beans,
    trimmed
zest and juice of 1 lime
lemon juice, to serve

CURRY BUTTER

3 tablespoons coconut oil
½ teaspoon ground ginger
½ teaspoon ground coriander
1 teaspoon garam masala
1 teaspoon ground cumin
½ teaspoon curry powder
¼ teaspoon chilli powder
½ teaspoon ground cinnamon
200 g (7 oz) salted butter

Remove the swordfish from the fridge 30 minutes prior to cooking.

For the curry butter, heat the coconut oil in a frying pan over medium heat. Add all the spices and lightly fry for 5 minutes or until aromatic. Remove from the heat and set aside to cool to room temperature.

Place the butter in a food processor and add the cooled spice mixture. Blitz for 20 seconds, or until combined.

Transfer the butter to an airtight container.

Season the fish and heat the coconut oil in a frying pan or chargrill pan over a medium–high heat. Add the fish steaks and cook for 1–2 minutes before adding ½ cup (125 g) of the curry butter (the rest can be stored in an airtight container in the fridge for up to 1 month).

Spoon the melted butter over the fish to coat. Cook for another 3 minutes before flipping the fish over and cooking on the other side for another 2–3 minutes, or until thoroughly cooked. Remove from the heat.

Meanwhile, bring a small saucepan of salted water to the boil and drop in the beans. Return to the boil and blanch the beans for 2–3 minutes before draining. Or you can chargrill the beans in a chargrill pan for about 8 minutes over a medium–high heat.

Taste the fish and adjust the seasoning, then finish with the lime zest and a squeeze of lemon or lime. Serve with the green beans.

Creamy Potato and Greens Salad with Zesty Anchovy Dressing

The key to any salad, really, is the dressing, and the dressing in this one is no different. It's sour, it's salty and it marries beautifully with comforting potatoes. Pair this salad with any barbecued meats or fish.

SERVES 4

500 g (1 lb 3 oz) baby potatoes, halved or quartered (if large)
4 eggs
80 g (2¾ oz) mixed salad greens, such as spinach, witlof (chicory) or rocket (arugula)
¼ cup (45 g) capers, drained and rinsed
8 anchovy fillets, chopped
¼ bunch dill, chopped
¼ bunch parsley, chopped

CREAMY DRESSING
½ cup (130 g) Greek-style yoghurt
1 tablespoon dijon mustard
2 teaspoons anchovy paste, or finely minced anchovies
50 ml (1¾ fl oz) lemon juice
1 garlic clove, minced
25 ml (¾ fl oz) extra-virgin olive oil
¼ bunch dill, finely chopped

Place the baby potatoes in a large saucepan and cover with water. Bring to the boil over high heat and cook the potatoes for 10–12 minutes, or until they are fork-tender. Drain, then place in a bowl and fill with cold water. Once cool, halve the potatoes.

While the potatoes are cooking and cooling, prepare the dressing. Whisk all of the ingredients together in a small bowl until well combined. Season with salt and pepper to taste.

Place the eggs in a small saucepan of cold water and bring to the boil over high heat. Allow to boil for 60 seconds before turning the heat off and letting the eggs cook in the residual heat for 6 minutes. Peel the eggs and set aside.

Transfer the potatoes to a large salad bowl. Add the mixed salad greens, capers, anchovies and herbs. Pour the dressing over the top and toss gently to combine.

Adjust the seasoning as needed. Finally, halve the eggs and place on top of the salad to serve.

Grilled Eggplant and Lentil Salad with Lemon-Mint Dressing

In botanical terms, eggplant (aubergine) is technically a fruit not a vegetable. In culinary terms, both eggplants and lentils have amazing utility, but they need big flavours to bring them to life, so don't skimp on the dressing here.

SERVES 2

2 medium eggplants
(aubergines), trimmed
and cut into wedges
2 tablespoons extra-virgin
olive oil
1 teaspoon ground cumin
1 teaspoon smoked paprika
1 cup (200 g) tinned green
or brown lentils, drained
and rinsed
1 cup (150 g) mixed cherry
tomatoes, halved
½ preserved lemon (optional),
roughly chopped
¼ cup (40 g) pine nuts, toasted
⅔ cup (100 g) crumbled feta
(optional)
¼ bunch mint leaves

LEMON-MINT DRESSING
¼ cup (60 ml) extra-virgin
olive oil
¼ cup (60 ml) lemon juice
1 teaspoon honey
¼ cup (15 g) mint leaves,
finely chopped
1 teaspoon dijon mustard

Preheat a barbecue or a chargrill pan to medium–high heat.

In a large mixing bowl, combine the eggplant, olive oil, cumin and paprika. Season and place on the hot barbecue or in the chargrill pan. Cook for 2–3 minutes on each side or until lightly charred. Remove from the heat and set aside.

Combine the ingredients for the dressing in a jar, seal and shake vigorously. Or you can whisk them by hand in a bowl. Season to taste with salt and pepper.

In a serving bowl or dish, combine the lentils, eggplant, tomatoes and preserved lemon, if using. Drizzle the dressing on top and toss lightly to mix.

Garnish with the toasted pine nuts, feta (if using) and mint leaves. Check and adjust the seasoning and serve.

Tuna Niçoise with Dill Lemon Mayonnaise

This is a fairly traditional recipe, but with a beautiful herby mayonnaise that slightly deviates from the usual vinaigrette. As with all our fish dishes, we recommend you look for the MSC (Marine Stewardship Council) certification (a blue tick on the label) to ensure you are buying seafood from fisheries that adhere to strict sustainability practices (see page 70).

SERVES 4

1 tablespoon extra-virgin
   olive oil
2 × 170 g (6 oz) Marine
   Stewardship Council–
   certified tuna steaks, or
   400 g (14 oz) tinned tuna
1 small red onion, sliced
8–10 small potatoes, boiled
   and quartered
150 g (5½ oz) green beans
4 large ripe tomatoes, cored
   and quartered
8–10 anchovy fillets
2 tablespoons capers,
   drained and rinsed
1 tablespoon finely chopped
   chives
4–5 tablespoons Lemon
   Mayonnaise (page 191)
2 × baby cos lettuces, trimmed
   and halved lengthways
lemon juice, to serve
4 eggs, boiled and halved

If you're using fresh tuna steaks, heat the olive oil in a frying pan over medium–high heat.

Place the steaks in the pan and cook for 1–2 minutes on each side, or until cooked to your liking (we like ours a little pink). Remove from the heat and set aside.

In a large mixing bowl, combine the onion, potato, beans, tomatoes, anchovies, capers and chives, and mix in the mayonnaise.

If you're using tinned tuna, add this to the mixture and lightly toss again.

Add the lettuce to a large serving bowl, top with the potato mixture and mix.

Lastly, if you're using tuna steaks, slice them into bite-sized cubes or strips, top with a squeeze of lemon juice and some salt and pepper, and add to the salad with the eggs.

Nourishing Green Elixir

This is something we have been selling through The Good Farm Shop from its earliest days, and folks love it. It's like WD40 for your body ... health in a cup! Essentially, you're pimping a beef-bone broth with a heap of nourishing greens for the ultimate health-inducing elixir. Bones are a rich source of marrow, and marrow contains collagen, which our bodies use to support an array of tissues. Plus, making your own broth is both cost-efficient and satisfying.

SERVES 12

3 kg (6 1b 12 oz) grass-finished beef bones
2 bay leaves
1 teaspoon whole black peppercorns
1 tablespoon apple cider vinegar
2 carrots, cut into segments
2 brown onions, peeled and quartered
1 cup (40 g) baby English spinach leaves
½ bunch Tuscan kale
1 head broccoli, trimmed
1 cup (20 g) parsley leaves
1 cup (130 g) frozen peas
100 g (3½ oz) salted butter
lemon juice, to serve

In a large stockpot, place the bones, bay leaves, peppercorns, vinegar, carrot and onion and cover with water. Season with salt and bring to the boil over high heat.

Once boiling, reduce the heat to a strong simmer, skimming off any impurities that rise to the surface. Once the impurities stop forming, put the lid on and cook over low heat for 12–24 hours, topping up the water as needed.

Remove from the heat and strain the broth into a clean pot. Discard the solids.

Place the broth back over medium heat and drop in the spinach, kale, broccoli, parsley, peas and butter. Cook for 10 minutes before removing from the heat, then blitz with a stick blender until emulsified.

Season and serve with a squeeze of lemon juice.

Roasted Butternut Pumpkin and Coconut Soup

This could be a winter warmer or a chilled summer appetiser. Pumpkin and coconut make a delicious pairing, creating a harmonious blend of autumnal flavours and tropical richness.

SERVES 4–6

1 large butternut pumpkin (squash), peeled, deseeded and cut into cubes
2 tablespoons extra-virgin olive oil, plus extra for drizzling
1 brown onion, roughly chopped
2 garlic cloves, roughly chopped
2–3 cm (¾–1¼ inch) piece ginger, peeled and finely chopped or grated
1 teaspoon ground cumin
1 teaspoon ground coriander
½ teaspoon ground turmeric
¼ teaspoon cayenne pepper
3 cups (750 ml) vegetable broth or stock
400 ml (14 fl oz) tin coconut cream
¼ bunch coriander (cilantro), leaves picked, to serve

Preheat the oven to 200°C (400°F).

Place the pumpkin on a baking tray. Drizzle with some olive oil and season with salt and pepper. Toss to coat the pumpkin evenly, then roast in the oven for 30–40 minutes, or until tender and lightly caramelised.

In a large stockpot, heat the olive oil over medium heat. Add the onion and cook until it becomes translucent, about 3–4 minutes.

Add the garlic and ginger and cook for another 2 minutes, then add the spices and stir well to coat the onion.

Add the cooked pumpkin, followed by the broth and bring to the boil over high heat. Reduce the heat to medium and simmer for 20 minutes.

Add the coconut cream and blend with a stick blender, or in batches in a benchtop blender.

Cook for another 2–3 minutes over medium heat, then season to taste with salt and pepper and serve with fresh coriander leaves.

Naked Cheeseburgers

Say goodbye to the bun and carbs and hello to some deliciousness without the dread of feeling too full. Don't be afraid to have a little pink in your patty (just as you might with a steak), which will mean allowing some extra time for the meat to rest after it comes off the barbecue or out of the pan.

SERVES 4

400 g (14 oz) minced (ground) beef (ideally 70% lean 30% fat)
½ brown onion, finely chopped
1 tablespoon thyme leaves, finely chopped
1 tablespoon extra-virgin olive oil
4 slices cheddar, large enough to cover a whole patty
16 iceberg lettuce leaves
4 tablespoons Barbecue Sauce (page 188)
4 tablespoons Avocado Butter (see below)
4–8 slices tomato
1 small red onion, thinly sliced
8 sliced dill pickles, to serve

AVOCADO BUTTER
1 ripe avocado, peeled, stone removed
1 teaspoon wholegrain mustard
splash of apple cider vinegar
¼ cup (15 g) basil leaves
1 tablespoon lemon juice
1 tablespoon extra-virgin olive oil

Remove the mince from the fridge 30 minutes before cooking.

Throw all the ingredients for the avocado butter in a blender and blitz for a few seconds until coarsely chopped. Transfer to a bowl and refrigerate until needed.

In a large mixing bowl, combine the mince, onion and thyme and season with salt and pepper.

Using your hands, mix the ingredients together, then divide into four evenly sized portions. Flatten into patties.

Heat the olive oil in a large frying pan over medium–high heat.

Once hot, season the beef patties and add to the hot pan. Cook for 3–5 minutes on each side (the cooking time will vary depending on the thickness of the patties). Once cooked through and nicely caramelised, remove from the heat and immediately top with the cheese so it can start to melt.

Assemble a burger by grabbing two lettuce leaves (these will be the base of the bun). Use the back of a tablespoon to spread 1 tablespoon of the avocado butter on top of the lettuce leaves.

Place a slice of tomato on top, followed by a patty, some onion and 1 tablespoon (or more, if you like) of the barbecue sauce. Complete the assembly by placing another two lettuce leaves on top for the lid. Serve with the pickle on the side.

Grab a large napkin and tuck it into your top – prepare to get messy!

Fragrant Cauliflower Rice Pilaf

Pilaf, also spelled pilau, pilaf or pulao, is a flavourful and aromatic rice dish that originated in the Middle East and Central Asia. It is hyper-adaptable, so feel free to swap in any ingredients you like, or use this one as a template for adding your own twist.

SERVES 4

2 tablespoons ghee or
   extra-virgin olive oil
1 brown onion, finely chopped
4 garlic cloves, minced
1 teaspoon ground cumin
1 teaspoon ground coriander
1 teaspoon ground turmeric
½ teaspoon ground cinnamon
¼ teaspoon cayenne pepper
1 head cauliflower, finely
   chopped or blitzed in a food
   processor to resemble rice
1½ cups (100 g) mixed
   vegetables (peas, carrots,
   capsicum/pepper), chopped
¼ cup (60 ml) veggie broth or
   stock, or water
juice of 1 lemon
¼ cup (40 g) toasted almonds,
   roughly chopped, to serve
¼ bunch coriander (cilantro),
   leaves chopped, to serve

Heat the ghee in a large frying pan over medium heat. Add the onion and sauté for 4–5 minutes.

Stir in the garlic and spices and cook for a further 2–3 minutes.

Add the riced cauliflower to the pan and stir well to coat with the spices. Add the mixed veggies and mix well.

Tip in the broth, season and reduce the heat to a gentle simmer. Continue cooking for 10–12 minutes, or until the veggies are tender.

Remove from the heat and allow to rest, covered, for a few minutes. Lift the lid, run a fork through the pilaf, and add the lemon juice, almonds and coriander. Season to taste and serve.

evenings

Beef Massaman Curry

This Thai curry is one of our consistent top sellers at The Good Farm Shop and one I make weekly at home. If you want more heat in the curry simply throw in a few more chillies, and you can always adjust the fish sauce, tamarind paste and sugar to taste at the end. Chuck is an amazingly versatile cut of beef, and reasonably priced compared to other more prized cuts. It has to be cooked low and long to ensure it tenderises.

SERVES 4

3 tablespoons coconut oil
3 red onions, sliced
4 tablespoons Massaman Paste
  (see below)
1 kg (2 lb 4 oz) chuck steak,
  diced
800 ml (28 fl oz) coconut cream
50 ml (1¾ fl oz) fish sauce
50 ml (1¾ fl oz) tamarind paste
50 g (1¾ oz) coconut sugar
200 g (7 oz) potatoes, cut into
  large cubes, or chunks
coriander (cilantro) leaves,
  to serve (optional)

MASSAMAN PASTE

2 cups (420 g) coconut oil
8 eschalots, peeled and
  quartered
125 g (4½ oz) whole dried
  chillies
20 garlic cloves, peeled
200 g (7 oz) ginger, peeled
3 teaspoons fennel seeds
2 teaspoons ground star anise
1 teaspoon ground cloves
3 teaspoons ground nutmeg
3 teaspoons ground cinnamon
3 teaspoons ground cumin
1 teaspoon ground turmeric

Place all the ingredients for the paste in a food processor or blender and blitz for 30 seconds, or until fully combined. Transfer to an airtight container and set aside. Any excess paste will keep for up to 2 weeks in the fridge.

Place a crock pot or Dutch oven over medium heat. Add the coconut oil and onion and sauté for 2–3 minutes. Add 4 heaped tablespoons of the paste and fry for 8–10 minutes, stirring often with a wooden spoon.

Add the beef and turn the heat up a little to brown the meat. Stir often to ensure the beef is browned all over.

Once browned, add the coconut cream and cook for 10 minutes. Add the fish sauce, tamarind and coconut sugar and stir.

Cover with the lid, drop the heat to low and cook for 1½–2 hours, or until the beef is tender. Stir occasionally.

Meanwhile, add the potatoes to a saucepan of salted water and bring to the boil. Reduce the heat and simmer for 15 minutes, or until the potatoes begin to soften. Remove from the heat and drain.

With 10 minutes cooking time remaining on the curry, add the potatoes to the pot to finish cooking. Mix through.

Once the beef is tender, remove from the heat but not before checking for a good balance of flavours: sourness (tamarind), saltiness (fish sauce) and sweetness (coconut sugar). Adjust accordingly, to taste. Garnish with coriander, if you like.

Rachel and Til's Fitzroy Chicken

When I was seventeen, I moved to Melbourne to follow in my parents' footsteps and study film and TV. It was bittersweet because I loved my new-found independence, but I really missed my mum, Rachel's, cooking. Luckily, she visited me a lot and on one occasion, she whipped out this recipe from a magazine and we cooked it in my little share house, much to my flatmates' enjoyment. We've added a few things to the recipe since then and it's been a favourite ever since.

SERVES 4–6

2 onions, peeled and quartered
5 garlic cloves
4 rosemary sprigs
4 chicken Marylands, skin on
1 chorizo sausage, cut into
    5 mm (¼ inch) slices
1 cup (250 ml) extra-virgin
    olive oil
2 cups (500 ml) red wine
    vinegar
1 cup (160 g) green Sicilian
    olives, pitted

Preheat the oven to 180°C (350°F).

Place the onion in a roasting tin with the garlic and rosemary sprigs.

Run your fingers between the chicken skin and thigh meat to ease the skin away from the meat (be careful not to tear it). Place the chorizo under the chicken skin.

Place the Marylands in the tray on top of the onion, garlic and rosemary.

Pour the olive oil and vinegar over the top and add the olives.

Season well with salt and pepper and bake for 35–45 minutes, or until the chicken is cooked through. Remove from the oven and allow to rest for 5 minutes before serving. Season to taste.

Serve with a simple garden salad and creamy mashed potatoes.

Easy Peri Peri Chicken

This recipe gets rolled out a lot in our house. The little kids haven't taken to it just yet, but they will in time ... and while we wait, there's more for Til, Tashi and me. We also sell this as a ready-to-use marinade at The Good Farm Shop – it's just so versatile.

SERVES 4

⅓ cup (80 ml) extra-virgin
  olive oil
6 garlic cloves, minced
2–3 cm (¾–1¼ inch) piece
  ginger, peeled and grated
1 teaspoon smoked paprika
1 teaspoon sweet paprika
½ teaspoon cayenne pepper
2 teaspoons dried oregano
juice of 1 lemon, plus extra
  for drizzling
800 g (1 lb 12 oz) boneless,
  skin-on chicken thighs
charred lemon halves,
  broccolini and radicchio
  wedges, to serve

In a large bowl, combine all the ingredients except the chicken, lemon halves, broccolini and radicchio. Mix thoroughly.

Add the chicken thighs and mix to ensure they are well coated with the sauce.

Preheat the oven to 190°C (375°F).

Heat a large ovenproof frying pan over medium heat and add the chicken. Cook the fillets for 3–4 minutes, or until the chicken is caramelised, before turning over and cooking for another 3–4 minutes on the other side. Transfer the pan to the oven and bake for 5–7 minutes until cooked through.

Transfer the chicken to a chopping board. Allow to rest for 3–4 minutes before roughly chopping.

Drizzle with some lemon juice, season and serve with charred lemon halves, broccolini and radicchio wedges.

Bryan's Steak and Chips with Black Olive Butter

It's slightly intimidating cooking for your father-in-law, but Bryan is a no-fuss kind of bloke – so it's not surprising this is his favourite meal. You can use the steak of your choice, but my favourites are scotch or rump due to their fat content, as this is where the flavour is. Grass-finished beef tends to have less marbling and fat coverage and has a yellow tinge to it.

SERVES 2

400 g (14 oz) floury potatoes, such as russet, peeled, rinsed and cut into 1.5 cm (⅝ inch) batons
100 ml (3½ fl oz) extra-virgin olive oil, plus 1 teaspoon extra for cooking the steak
1 teaspoon dried rosemary
2 steaks (eye fillet, scotch fillet, T-bone and rump are excellent choices)
2 tablespoons Black Olive Butter (page 194)

Bring a saucepan of salted water to the boil and drop in the potatoes. Return to the boil before reducing the heat to a steady simmer for 12 minutes. Drain, and lightly toss them in the colander to 'rough up' the surface of the potato. Place in a container (uncovered) and freeze for 1–2 hours.

Once the potatoes have chilled, preheat the oven to 220°C (425°F).

Place the olive oil in a baking dish with the dried rosemary and put in the oven for 5 minutes before adding the potatoes.

Return the dish to the oven and bake for 30–40 minutes, or until golden, turning a few times to ensure the chips are evenly crisp.

Remove the steaks from the fridge and set aside.

With about 10 minutes left on the chips, place a heavy-based frying pan over high heat.

Season both sides of the steaks. Add the extra olive oil to the pan and, once hot, add the steaks. If your steak is about 2 cm (¾ in) thick, cook them for around 3 minutes on each side for medium rare (adjust the cooking time depending on the thickness of the steak and how you like it cooked). Don't move the steaks for the first 3 minutes – this will create a lovely caramelised crust. Once this has developed, turn them over.

With 1 minute remaining on the steaks, add 1 tablespoon of the butter to the pan and baste the steaks with it. Once cooked to your liking, remove the steaks from the pan and rest for 2–3 minutes. Remove the chips from the oven and season.

Place the steak on a serving plate and top with the remaining butter. Serve with the chips and a green salad, if you like.

Til's Veggie Curry

When I first met Til she had been a vegetarian and vegan, and so had developed a repertoire of veggie dishes. This one is a cracker. We used it in The Good Farm Shop from day one and it remains one of the best sellers (but if any customers ask ... it's my recipe, of course). One of the most important considerations when cooking curries or dishes with spices is to allow the spices to fry off or cook through to remove their harshness.

SERVES 4–5

¼ Kent pumpkin (squash), peeled and cut into 2 cm (¾ inch) cubes
2 sweet potatoes, peeled and cut into 2 cm (¾ inch) cubes
2 large white potatoes, peeled and cut into 2 cm (¾ inch) cubes
1 head cauliflower, cut into small florets
6 tablespoons coconut oil
2 small red onions, sliced
4 garlic cloves, minced
2 cm (¾ inch) piece ginger, peeled and minced
1 tablespoon garam masala
½ teaspoon chilli flakes
1 teaspoon ground turmeric
2 × 400 g (14 oz) tins diced tomatoes
2 × 400 ml (14 fl oz) tins coconut cream
400 g (14 oz) tin chickpeas, drained and rinsed
2 bunches English spinach, roughly chopped
Greek-style or plain yoghurt, to serve

Preheat the oven to 180°C (350°F).

In a large roasting tin, spread the pumpkin, potatoes and cauliflower (you may need two trays). Melt half the coconut oil and drizzle it on top of the vegetables, then season well.

Bake for 40 minutes, or until softened and browned, then remove from the heat and set aside.

Meanwhile, heat the remaining coconut oil in a frying pan over medium heat and add the onion, garlic and ginger. Fry for 2–3 minutes before adding the spices and stirring with a wooden spoon. Cook for another 10 minutes.

Add the tinned tomatoes and coconut cream and bring to the boil. Knock back the heat to a simmer, then add the chickpeas and cook for 25 minutes.

Add the spinach and roasted veggies and cook for another 10 minutes, or until the veggies are hot.

Season to taste and serve with a dollop of yoghurt.

Slow-cooked Lamb Shoulder with Beer

Good friends of ours recently produced their own beer and dropped some around to us to try. Most would have drunk it in homage to said friends (and I did that too), but I decided to put it to use in this delicious lamb shoulder recipe. The trick with slow cooking is to ensure the meat is sufficiently (about 80 per cent) covered by liquid – broth, tomatoes, wine, beer, etc. Remember that the meat will typically release liquid as it cooks, too.

SERVES 6–8

1.5 kg (3 lb 5 oz) bone-in
   lamb shoulder
2 tablespoons extra-virgin
   olive oil
1 tinny of your favourite beer
2 brown onions, trimmed
   and peeled
6 large tomatoes, stalks
   removed
1 red capsicum (pepper),
   destemmed and cored
6 garlic cloves, peeled
1 tablespoon rosemary leaves
2 teaspoons dried oregano
1 tablespoon honey
pinch of sea salt
pinch of ground black pepper

Preheat the oven to 160°C (315°F).

Place a Dutch oven or ovenproof casserole dish over medium-high heat. Season the lamb generously with salt and pepper.

Add the olive oil to the Dutch oven, place the lamb in the dish and brown on all sides to seal the meat. This should only take 2–3 minutes on each side.

Once the lamb is browned, pour the beer into the dish to deglaze it. Bubble for 3–4 minutes to allow the alcohol to burn off.

Meanwhile, add the remaining ingredients to a blender and blitz for 20–30 seconds. Pour this over the lamb and cover the dish with the lid before popping in the oven. Cook for 3 hours, turning the dish every 45 minutes or so.

After 3 hours the lamb should be falling away from the bone. Remove from the oven and carefully transfer the sauce from the dish into a large saucepan set over high heat. Reduce the sauce by 25 per cent, then season to taste. Once reduced, pour the sauce back over the lamb and serve.

Tashi's Butter Chicken

Indian is, hands down, my favourite cuisine, and since he was old enough to hold his head up, Tashi has enjoyed many an Indian feast too. However, for the first ten years of his life the only Indian dish he would eat was butter chicken, so this recipe is an ode to him. He now loves other Indian dishes, thankfully, but this is a goodie! This recipe works just as well if you replace the almonds with cashew nuts. Personally, I don't blend the curry as I like to see textures in my food, but if you're looking for authenticity, blend it up.

SERVES 4

800 g (1 lb 12 oz) skinless, boneless chicken thighs
4 tablespoons coconut oil
1 large brown onion, sliced
6 garlic cloves, minced
2 cm (¾ inch) piece ginger, peeled and minced
2 teaspoons ground turmeric
1 tablespoon garam masala
1 teaspoon mild chill powder
1 teaspoon ground coriander
½ teaspoon ground cloves
1 teaspoon ground cumin
1.2 kg (2 lb 12 oz) tinned diced tomatoes
400 ml (14 fl oz) tin coconut cream
1 cup (125 g) slivered almonds
150 g (5½ oz) butter
1 cup (250 ml) thick (double) cream

Remove the thighs from the fridge 30 minutes before cooking.

Heat 2 tablespoons of the coconut oil in a large frying pan over high heat and add the chicken thighs (in batches, if necessary). Cook for 15 minutes, turning regularly, or until well browned and cooked through. Once cooked, set aside. Tip the pan juices into a large saucepan.

Add the remaining coconut oil to the saucepan and set it over medium heat.

Add the onion, garlic and ginger and fry for 2–3 minutes before adding the spices and frying for 10 minutes, stirring often.

Add the tomatoes, coconut cream and almonds and bring to the boil. Reduce to a simmer and cook for 25 minutes.

Roughly chop the chicken thighs and add them to the pot.

Add the butter and cream and simmer for another 10 minutes.

Season to taste before blending with a stick blender (optional) until smooth and all the nuts have been processed. Serve with your favourite curry accompaniments.

Mustard Rubbed Rib-eye Steak with Mint Salsa Verde

This is stand-out recipe for its simplicity but also for its wow factor. Family and friends will drop their jaws when this hits the table. The salsa verde is the perfect accompaniment to beef and the tartness cuts through the fattiness of the rib eye. Enjoy!

SERVES 4

1 rib-eye steak
  (approx. 900 g/2 lb),
  at room temperature
2 tablespoons dijon mustard
1 tablespoon extra-virgin
  olive oil
Salsa Verde (page 188),
  to serve

Remove the steak from the fridge at least 30 minutes before cooking. Fire up the barbecue to high heat or get a chargrill pan nice and hot on the stove.

Using your hands or the back of a spoon, rub the mustard all over the steak. Generously season the steak with salt and pepper.

Lightly brush the steak with the olive oil before laying it into the pan or onto the barbecue. First, lay the steak on its fatty edge for 1–2 minutes to render the fat to cook with.

After 3–4 minutes, lay the steak on its side. Depending on the thickness of the rib eye, cook each side for 7–9 minutes until beautifully caramelised and medium rare.

Serve with the salsa verde.

Steak and Kidney Pie with Buttery Colcannon

Folks would drive miles to eat my mum's steak and kidney pie. The pub car park would be full before the doors even opened. I really hope this version does her proud (love you, Mum x).

SERVES 4

6 tablespoons extra-virgin olive oil
2 large brown onions, chopped
8 garlic cloves, minced
2 tablespoons dried thyme
2 tablespoons dried oregano
2 tablespoons dried basil
¼ cup (60 g) tomato paste (concentrated purée)
900 g (2 lb) chuck steak, diced
300 g (10½ oz) beef kidney, trimmed and diced (similar size as the chuck)
1.4 litres (47 fl oz) passata
200 g (7 oz) Swiss brown mushrooms, sliced
grated cheese, for topping (optional)

COLCANNON
1.2 kg (2 lb 12 oz) floury potatoes, such as Dutch creams, peeled, washed and roughly chopped
½ green cabbage, shredded
200 g (7 oz) salted butter

Preheat the oven to 160°C (315°F).

Heat the olive oil in an ovenproof baking dish (one that has a lid and can double as a pie dish) over medium heat. Add the onion and garlic and sauté for 5–6 minutes.

Add the herbs and stir with a wooden spoon.

After another 5 minutes, add the tomato paste and stir through the onion mix.

Add the chuck and kidney and stir as they brown. Cook for another 5 minutes before adding the passata, then stir through and season with salt and pepper.

Cover with the lid and transfer to the oven. Cook for 1½–2 hours, stirring every 45 minutes or so.

Place the potatoes in a large saucepan of salted water and bring to the boil over high heat. Once boiling, drop the heat to a steady simmer and cook for 35 minutes, or until the potatoes are soft. Add the cabbage and cook for another 6 minutes, then remove from the heat and drain.

Transfer the potato and cabbage to a bowl, add the salted butter and mash until smooth. Season to taste with salt and pepper, then set side.

Add the mushrooms to the beef mixture about 45 minutes before the end of the cooking time. Stir to mix well, then cover and return to the oven to finish cooking.

Remove the steak and kidney from the oven and use a spoon or palette knife to put the mash on top and level it out. (Add some grated cheese, if you wish.)

Return the dish to the oven for another 20 minutes, or until the potato is golden on top. Remove and serve.

Slow-cooked Barbecue Beef Ribs with Caramelised Onions

The beautiful thing about the farm is the affinity that all members of the Brown family, both immediate and distant, feel for it. Everyone is welcome. This recipe came about during a long weekend when cousins and second cousins descended upon Nambucca Valley for food, connection, surfing and wintry fires – our version of heaven on earth.

SERVES 6–8

2 tablespoons extra-virgin
  olive oil
2 kg (4 lb 8 oz) beef short ribs
6 eschalots, peeled and sliced
400 ml (14 fl oz) Barbecue
  Sauce (page 188)
Caramelised Onions (page 193),
  to serve

Preheat the oven to 150°C (300°F).

Heat the oil for the beef ribs in a Dutch oven or crock pot over high heat. Add the beef ribs, two or three at a time, and turn to brown all over.

Once browned, return all the ribs to the pot with the eschalots and pour in 300 ml (10½ fl oz) of the barbecue sauce, leaving 100 ml (3½ fl oz) for the end of the cooking.

Cover with the lid and cook in the oven for 3 hours, or until the beef is falling away from the bone.

With 20 minutes of cooking time remaining for the ribs, heat the remaining barbecue sauce in a saucepan over low heat until warmed through.

Remove the ribs from the oven and transfer to a serving dish. Pour the heated barbecue sauce over the top and serve with the caramelised onions and a green salad.

Warm Cauliflower Salad with Sweet Potato Purée

This is warming and comforting without the stodge. Cauliflowers come in a few varieties and colours, so feel free to use an orange, purple or green one for more vibrancy, if you like.

SERVES 4

1–1.2 kg (2 lb 4 oz–2 lb 12 oz) sweet potatoes, peeled and roughly chopped
1 head cauliflower, stalk and leaves removed, cut into small florets
3 large red onions, peeled and segmented
4 tablespoons extra-virgin olive oil
1 tablespoon ground cumin, plus 1 teaspoon extra
1 tablespoon za'atar
1 tablespoon butter
400 g (14 oz) tin chickpeas, drained and rinsed
¼ bunch mint leaves, to serve
1 bunch parsley leaves, to serve
150 g (5½ oz) feta cheese, to serve

DRESSING
½ cup (130 g) plain yoghurt
juice of 1 lemon
¼ cup (15 g) chopped dill
½ teaspoon sumac

Preheat the oven to 190°C (375°F).

Place the sweet potatoes in a saucepan, cover with salted water and bring to the boil. Cook for 30 minutes, or until softened, then drain and transfer to a blender or food processor.

To a roasting tin, add the cauliflower, red onion, 3 tablespoons of the olive oil, cumin and za'atar and lightly toss. Season and roast in the oven for 30–35 minutes, or until the cauliflower is lightly browned. Remove and set aside.

Combine the dressing ingredients in a bowl and season to taste.

Add the remaining olive oil, butter and extra cumin to the sweet potato and blitz to a purée. Season to taste, then spread the purée over a serving plate.

In a large mixing bowl, gently combine the roasted cauliflower and onion with the chickpeas and the yoghurt dressing.

Arrange on top of the purée and sprinkle the fresh herbs and feta on top. Season and serve.

Campfire-roasted Pumpkin with Spiced Maple Glaze

An open fire is a prerequisite during a stay on the farm. It wards off the mozzies in summer, keeps you warm in winter and always adds atmosphere. This is a great (and simple) recipe to add to the campfire cook-up. That's not to say you can't have it on a night in: just cook it in the oven at 190°C (375°F).

SERVES 8–10

1 whole Jap pumpkin (squash)
2 tablespoons extra-virgin
  olive oil
¼ cup (60 ml) maple syrup,
  or honey
1 teaspoon ground cinnamon
½ teaspoon ground nutmeg
¼ teaspoon ground cloves

Once the campfire has died down to hot coals, cut the pumpkin in half and scoop out the seeds and pulp using a spoon. Cut into generous chunks or slices.

Combine the olive oil, maple syrup and spices in a large mixing bowl, then brush the glaze on to the pumpkin. Season well with salt and pepper.

Place the pumpkin directly on the hot coals using some long tongs.

Leave until the pumpkin caramelises on one side, then gently turn to caramelise all sides. It should take about 20 minutes to cook through.

Remove from the heat and allow to cool before serving.

Fish Pie

This is a super tasty recipe for lunch or dinner and perfect to feed the fam and a few friends. If you've got a full house, simply add more sauce and fish. Special note to our very first employee at The Good Farm Shop, chef Lauren, who came up with the superb topping. We usually use MSC ling for this dish, but any firm white fish will work just as well.

SERVES 4–6

1 ear of corn, outer leaves removed
2 tablespoons extra-virgin olive oil
2 large red onions, finely chopped
2 eschalots, finely sliced
½ bunch fresh parsley, stalks and leaves finely chopped separately
350 ml (12 fl oz) dry white wine
75 g (2¾ oz) salted butter
200 ml (7 fl oz) full-cream milk
150 ml (5 fl oz) thick (double) cream
1 tablespoon brown rice flour, to thicken (optional)
500 g (1 lb 2 oz) white fish (such as flathead or ling), cut into rough 3 cm (1¼ inch) cubes
300 g (10½ oz) smoked mackerel, flaked and bones removed
½ cup (30 g) finely chopped dill

CRUMB TOPPING
¾ cup (120 g) almonds
½ cup (75 g) pepitas (pumpkin seeds)
2 tablespoons dried dill
2 tablespoons dried tarragon
150 g (5½ oz) grated cheddar

Throw all the ingredients for the crumb topping in a food processor and blitz for 10–12 seconds, or until a 'crumb' forms. Transfer to a bowl, season and set aside.

Bring a saucepan of salted water to the boil, add the corn and cook on a rapid simmer for 10 minutes. Remove from the heat, drain and leave to cool, then cut off the kernels. Set aside.

Heat the oil in a large saucepan over medium heat and add the onion, eschalot and parsley stalks. Sauté for 10 minutes, or until the onion has softened and become translucent.

Add the wine and increase the heat to high for 2–3 minutes to cook off the alcohol before returning the heat to medium. Add the butter, milk and cream, and stir through.

Add the rice flour, if using, and stir until it thickens, then add the fish and corn and stir through.

Add the smoked fish and stir again. Return to a simmer and cook for 8–10 minutes, or until the white fish is cooked through.

Preheat the oven to 160°C (315°F).

Add the chopped dill and parsley leaves to the fish mixture and stir through for 1 minute.

Remove from the heat and transfer the mixture to a pie dish. Sprinkle the crumb in an even layer on top and bake in the oven for 15–20 minutes, or until the crumb is golden.

Remove from the oven and serve.

Bangers, Mash and Onion Gravy

Healthy food doesn't have to be alfalfa sprouts and mung beans, it can be familiar and comforting and this recipe epitomises that. Sausages are a crucial cut in the nose-to-tail approach, using leftover fat and trim from the butchering process. There's no hiding my British roots with this recipe, either. Lean beef or chicken sausages can lack fat and, therefore, flavour, so make sure you select a gluten-free sausage with a good amount of fat in it.

SERVES 4–6

8–12 pork or beef sausages
1 tablespoon extra-virgin
   olive oil

ONION GRAVY
2 tablespoons olive oil
2 large brown onions, thinly
   sliced
75 ml (2½ fl oz) balsamic
   vinegar
2 cups (500 ml) beef broth
   or stock
1 cup (250 ml) red wine
1 teaspoon dijon mustard
3 thyme sprigs
1 rosemary sprig
2 tablespoons besan (chickpea
   flour), or brown rice flour
   (optional)

MASH
600 kg (1 lb 5 oz) sweet
   potatoes, peeled and
   chopped
600 kg (1 lb 5 oz) Dutch cream
   potatoes, peeled and
   chopped
2 tablespoons butter
a splash of milk (optional)

Remove the sausages from the fridge 30 minutes before cooking.

Heat the oil for the onion gravy in a saucepan over medium heat and sauté the onion for 5–6 minutes.

Add the balsamic vinegar and cook for another 3–4 minutes before covering the pan with a lid and reducing the heat to low. Cook for another 20 minutes before setting aside.

Meanwhile, bring the broth to the boil in a saucepan and cook until it reduces by half. Add the wine, mustard and herbs and continue to reduce. Pass the gravy through a fine-mesh sieve into a clean saucepan.

Once reduced you can add the flour to help thicken the gravy if you wish. Add a pinch of salt, then gently whisk it in and leave to cook over low heat while you prepare the mash and sausages.

Add the chopped potatoes to a saucepan of salted water and bring to the boil over high heat. Simmer rapidly until cooked through, then drain. Transfer to a bowl, add the butter (and milk, if using), then mash with a fork or masher. Season to taste with salt and pepper.

Heat the tablespoon of olive oil in a large frying pan and cook the sausages over medium–high heat for 10 minutes (depending on the thickness of the sausages), or until browned and cooked through.

Add the onions to the gravy and stir, then pour the gravy over the sausages in the pan and put over a low heat for a few minutes to warm through. Serve with the mash.

Til's Spiced Red Lentil Dahl

If you read my food story on page 21, you'll know that during my twenties I was mostly vegan and vegetarian. It wasn't until I met Scott that I started eating meat again. As a non-meat-eater, I would cook a lot with red lentils, adding whatever ingredients I had on hand. I didn't realise it at the time, but I was essentially making dahl. Red lentils have quite a bit of flavour on their own, but I quickly realised that adding spices elevated them to something really special.

SERVES 4

1 cup (205 g) red lentils,
    rinsed and drained
4 cups (1 litre) vegetable broth
    or stock
2 tablespoons coconut oil
1 onion, finely chopped
3 garlic cloves, minced
2.5 cm (1 inch) piece ginger,
    peeled and grated
1 teaspoon ground turmeric
1 teaspoon ground cumin
1 teaspoon ground coriander
1 teaspoon curry powder
½ teaspoon ground cinnamon
¼ teaspoon cayenne pepper,
    or to taste
400 g (14 oz) tin diced tomatoes
400 ml (14 fl oz) tin coconut
    milk
2 cups (130 g) chopped English
    spinach
juice of 1 lemon, plus extra
    to serve (optional)
coriander (cilantro) and
    Greek-style yoghurt, to serve

In a large saucepan, combine the lentils and vegetable broth. Bring to the boil, then reduce the heat to a simmer and cook for 15–20 minutes, or until the lentils are soft and cooked through. Skim any foam that rises to the surface.

In a separate large frying pan, heat the coconut oil over medium heat. Add the onion, garlic and ginger and sauté until the onion is translucent, about 5–7 minutes.

Stir in the spices and cook for another minute to release their flavours.

Add the cooked lentils and stir to combine and let the flavours meld for a few minutes.

Pour in the diced tomato and coconut milk and stir again until well combined.

Bring the mixture to a gentle simmer and cook for 10–15 minutes, allowing the flavours to blend and the sauce to thicken slightly.

Stir in the chopped spinach, allowing it to wilt in the dahl. Squeeze in the lemon juice and give it a final stir, then season to taste.

To serve, ladle the fragrant dahl into bowls, garnish with fresh coriander leaves and dollop on some yoghurt. You can finish with another squeeze of lemon if you like.

Our French Restaurant Dinner (Steak au Poivre with Roasted Chat Potatoes and Cafe de Paris Butter)

Before Til and I had kids – and even when Zan was a bub – we used to frequent a local traditional French restaurant in Avalon. It's one of those places where the menu never changes ... and for good reason. It's consistently spot-on. For now, we have to settle for home-made versions of our favourite dishes until the little kids are civilised enough not to throw Dad's snails across the room.

SERVES 2

10–12 chat potatoes, washed
4 tablespoons extra-virgin
    olive oil
2 eye fillet steaks, at room
    temperature
1 tablespoon butter
blanched green beans, to serve
garden salad, to serve

PEPPERCORN SAUCE
1 tablespoon extra-virgin
    olive oil
1 tablespoon salted butter
2 eschalots, finely chopped
4 garlic cloves, finely chopped
3 tablespoons brandy
1 tablespoon dijon mustard
½ cup (125 ml) beef broth
    or stock
2 tablespoons green
    peppercorns in brine, drained
200 ml (7 fl oz) thick (double)
    cream

Add the potatoes to a saucepan of salted water and bring to the boil. Reduce to a steady simmer and cook for 20–25 minutes, or until soft. Drain and set aside.

Preheat the oven to 200°C (400°F).

Add 3 tablespoons of the olive oil to a roasting tin and pop in the oven for 10 minutes.

Using the back of a spoon, lightly press down on the cooked potatoes to crush them a little. Don't worry if they lose their form.

Transfer the potatoes to the roasting tin and stir to coat in the hot oil. Return to the oven for 40 minutes, or until browned and crispy, turning halfway through.

Now on to the peppercorn sauce. Heat the olive oil and butter in a small saucepan over medium heat and add the eschalot and garlic. Sauté for 6 minutes or until softened.

Add the brandy and allow the alcohol to burn off, about 3–4 minutes. Next, add the mustard and broth and simmer for 10 minutes.

Add the peppercorns and stir through, then add the cream and return to a simmer for 8 minutes.

Season and set aside.

CAFE DE PARIS BUTTER
2 tablespoons extra-virgin
   olive oil
½ brown onion, roughly
   chopped
1 teaspoon curry powder
½ cup (125 g) salted butter,
   roughly chopped
1 teaspoon capers, drained
   and rinsed
1 anchovy fillet
½ cup (10 g) parsley leaves
10 tarragon leaves
juice of 1 lemon

To make the Cafe de Paris butter, heat the olive oil over low heat in a small frying pan. Add the onion and curry powder and stir to combine, then cook for 15–20 minutes, or until the onion has softened. Remove from the heat and set aside to cool.

Place the cooked onions and remaining butter ingredients in a food processor and blitz for 60 seconds or until smooth. Season to taste with salt and pepper and adjust with a little more lemon juice if necessary. Transfer to a bowl and set aside.

Now it's time for the steak. Season both sides well with salt and pepper. Heat the remaining tablespoon of olive oil in a frying pan over high heat. Once hot, add the steak to the pan and caramelise for 2–3 minutes (resist any temptation to move the steak during this time) before turning it over and doing the same on the other side. With 1 minute of cooking time remaining, add the butter to the pan and baste the steak. Turn the steak a few more times to get good colourisation, then remove from the pan and set aside to rest.

Meanwhile, warm the peppercorn sauce and remove the potatoes from the oven and season.

Once the steak has rested for 3–4 minutes, serve with a generous spoonful of peppercorn sauce, the crispy potatoes and a knob of Cafe de Paris butter. Season and serve with blanched green beans and garden salad.

Braised Lamb Neck Rogan Josh

Prior to selling ready meals, The Good Farm Shop was an online butcher store selling beautiful regeneratively raised produce. One of the perks of this business was squirrelling away certain cuts that were somewhat less desirable or understood. Lamb necks were always the first to be tucked away. It is a delicious cut, similar to oxtail in many respects, and never disappoints.

SERVES 4–6

1 tablespoon coconut oil
2 brown onions, chopped
1.8–2 kg (4–4 lb 8 oz) lamb
  necks
2 × 400 g (14 oz) tins diced
  tomatoes
1½ cups (390 g) Greek-style
  or plain yoghurt
¼ bunch coriander (cilantro),
  leaves picked, to serve

ROGAN JOSH PASTE

1 tablespoon fennel seeds
2 tablespoons ground cumin
2 tablespoons ground coriander
2 tablespoons paprika
1 tablespoon ground turmeric
1 tablespoon Kashmiri chilli
  powder, or regular chilli
  powder
1 tablespoon ground cinnamon
1 tablespoon ground cardamon
1 tablespoon ground cloves
1 tablespoon ground black
  pepper
2 cm (¾ in) piece fresh ginger,
  peeled
10 garlic cloves, peeled
6 eschalots, peeled and
  roughly chopped
1 teaspoon ground nutmeg
1 cup (210 g) coconut oil

Start with the rogan josh paste. Lightly toast the fennel seeds in a dry frying pan over medium heat until they release their aroma. Be careful not to burn them. Remove from the heat and let them cool.

In a spice grinder or with a mortar and pestle, grind the toasted fennel seeds into a fine powder.

Place all the ingredients, including the fennel, in a blender or food processor and blitz until smooth and fully combined. Transfer to an airtight container.

Preheat the oven to 140°C (275°F).

Heat the tablespoon of coconut oil in a large ovenproof dish over medium heat and add the onion and 3 tablespoons of the rogan josh paste. Sauté for 10 minutes, stirring often. (Leftover paste will keep in the fridge for up to 1 month in an airtight container.)

Once the onion has softened, add the lamb necks and mix to coat the lamb in the paste.

Add the tomatoes and yoghurt and stir.

Cover and place in the oven for 3 hours, giving the mixture a stir two or three times throughout the cooking.

Remove from the oven and transfer to a serving dish. Garnish with fresh coriander and serve.

Bryan's One-hit Wonder

There's a running joke in the Brown household that this is the only dish Bryan can cook. Well ... this, and a chop on the barbie. Apparently he came up with this recipe one night when Rachel was out and it was a complete fluke that it turned out so delicious. I don't think he's made it since, but we quite enjoy it.

SERVES 4

2 tablespoons extra-virgin olive oil
8 skinless, boneless chicken thighs
2 tablespoons wholegrain mustard
2 tablespoons honey
1 cup (250 ml) thick (double) cream, plus extra if needed
blanched green beans and asparagus, to serve

Heat the olive oil in a frying pan over medium heat. Add the chicken and brown on both sides.

Turn the heat down to low and spread the mustard over the chicken, followed by the honey.

Cook for another 5 minutes, then pour in the cream. Cover the pan and cook for about 10 minutes, or until the chicken is cooked through. You may need to add more cream if the liquid starts to evaporate.

Serve with green beans and asparagus.

Barramundi and Crispy Rosemary Potatoes with Spicy Romesco Sauce

The magic of these crispy potatoes is in the imperfection. Don't worry if they lose their shape – this simply creates the most amazing crispy nibbles.

When you're shopping for your fish, look for the MSC (Marine Stewardship Council) certification (see page 70). There are some great and sustainable barramundi farms in Australia and Asia, such as Humpy Doo Barramundi - it's just a matter of asking your fishmonger or searching online.

SERVES 4

4 × 200 g (7 oz) barramundi
    fillets, skin on
1 kg (2 lb 4 oz) chat potatoes,
    washed
90 ml (3 fl oz) extra-virgin olive
    oil, plus 1 tablespoon extra
    for frying
2–4 rosemary sprigs
juice of ¼ lemon
Spicy Romesco Sauce
    (page 191), to serve

Remove the fish from the fridge 30 minutes before cooking.

Place the potatoes in a saucepan of salted water and bring to the boil. Reduce the heat and simmer for 20 minutes, or until softened, then drain.

Crush the potatoes using the bottom of a saucepan or frying pan and allow to cool.

Preheat the oven to 220°C (425°F).

Place the oil and rosemary in a roasting tin and place in the oven to heat. Once hot, remove from the oven and gently tip in the crushed potatoes. Season and return the tin to the oven for 35–40 minutes, or until the potatoes are browned and crispy.

Pat the fish dry with paper towel, then season. Heat the extra olive oil in a frying pan over medium–high heat and place the fish in the oil, skin side down. Hold it down with a spatula for the first few moments to prevent the fish curling. Cook for 4–5 minutes without moving the fish.

Once browned and crispy, flip the fillet to the flesh side and cook for a further 2–3 minutes (depending on the thickness), or until the fish can be flaked easily with a fork.

Remove from the heat, drizzle with the lemon juice, season and allow to rest.

Heat the Romesco sauce in a small saucepan.

Check on the potatoes – if they're nicely crispy, remove them from the oven and transfer to a serving bowl, season and squeeze a little lemon juice over the top.

Serve with the barramundi and spicy Romesco sauce.

Chicken and Tarragon Scalloped Pie

This dish is similar to one that we sell at The Good Farm Shop that flies out the door. It's the perfect recipe for a low-key dinner party with friends, and works equally well with a split of chicken breast and thigh meat. The scalloped topping gives the dish a wonderful look and I guarantee it will be devoured with gusto.

SERVES 8

10 waxy potatoes, such as Yukon Gold, peeled
1.5 kg (3 lb 5 oz) skinless, boneless chicken thighs, at room temperature
2 tablespoons extra-virgin olive oil
1 teaspoon butter
3 carrots, diced
2 red onions, diced
4 garlic cloves, minced
6 eschalots, trimmed and sliced
½ cup (30 g) finely chopped tarragon
½ cup (30 g) finely chopped parsley
3 cups (750 ml) chicken broth or stock
300 ml (10½ fl oz) thick (double) cream
1 tablespoon arrowroot or brown rice flour
1 cup (130 g) frozen peas

Place the potatoes in a large pot of salted water and bring to the boil. Cook until tender but still holding their shape, then remove from the heat and drain. Refrigerate to cool while you make the filling.

Preheat the oven to 180°C (350°F).

Season the chicken thighs and heat the olive oil in a large frying pan over high heat. Add the chicken to the pan, skin side down, and cook for 2–3 minutes on each side to lightly brown and seal the chicken. Remove from the heat and set aside to cool.

Reduce the heat to medium. To the same pan add the butter, carrot, onion, garlic and eschalot and sauté for 5–6 minutes, stirring often. Add a little more olive oil if you think it's going to catch.

Add the fresh herbs and stir through before adding the broth and bringing to a strong simmer. Add the cream and bring back to a simmer, then add the arrowroot flour and lightly whisk until the mixture thickens.

Chop the chicken into generous chunks and stir them through the sauce.

Add the peas and stir for 5 minutes, then season and remove from the heat. Transfer the mixture to a pie dish.

Cut the potatoes into 5 mm (½ inch) slices and layer over the top of the pie mixture. Season and bake in the oven for 30 minutes, or until the potato has browned. Remove from the heat, season and serve.

66 Some people bought from
us because they were gung-ho
about the environment, some
were health focused and
others really cared about
the way animals were treated.

Beef Cheek Rendang

There was a time when beef cheek was one of the cheapest cuts available, but in the past few years people have discovered how absolutely delicious it is, and the price now reflects that. For me, its the way it melts in your mouth when cooked to perfection. It is the ultimate prime cut. And let's not forget there are only two per beast, so consider this dish extra special.

SERVES 4–6

1 tablespoon coconut oil
4–6 beef cheeks
2 × 400 ml (14 fl oz) tins coconut milk
5 makrut lime leaves
2 × 5–6 cm (2–2½ inch) cinnamon sticks
3 green cardamom pods
3 whole cloves
3 whole star anise
2 tablespoons tamarind paste
2 tablespoons coconut sugar
¾ cup (65 g) desiccated coconut
2 tablespoons fish sauce
⅓ bunch coriander (cilantro), leaves picked, to serve

RENDANG PASTE

6 eschalots, peeled and halved
4 garlic cloves, peeled
3 cm (1¼ inch) piece ginger, peeled and roughly chopped
3 lemongrass stalks, white parts only, chopped
3 red chillies, destemmed
1 tablespoon ground coriander
1 tablespoon ground cumin
1 tablespoon ground turmeric
½ teaspoon ground cloves
¼ nutmeg, finely grated
2–3 tablespoons coconut oil

Preheat the oven to 140°C (275°F).

For the paste, combine all the ingredients in a food processor and blitz to a smooth paste. Add some more coconut oil if needed to achieve a paste-like consistency. Transfer to a bowl and set aside.

In a large, heavy-based pot or Dutch oven, heat the coconut oil over medium–high heat and sear the beef cheeks in batches until browned on all sides. Set aside.

To the same pot, add the rendang paste and sauté for 1–2 minutes until fragrant.

Return the seared beef cheeks to the pot and stir to coat with the paste. Pour in the coconut milk and add the makrut lime leaves and whole spices.

Cover with a lid and place in the oven for 3–4 hours, or until the meat is tender and the sauce has thickened. Stir occasionally to prevent sticking.

Finally, stir in the tamarind paste, coconut sugar, desiccated coconut and fish sauce. Taste and adjust the seasoning, then continue to simmer for another 30 minutes to allow the flavours to meld before removing from the heat and serving with fresh coriander leaves.

Moussaka

One of my earliest memories is indulging in moussaka and halloumi on a holiday in Cyprus. Heaven. Our moussaka is a crowd favourite and this version is dinner-party worthy.

SERVES 10

4 eggplants (aubergines), trimmed and cut into 1 cm (½ in) slices
4 tablespoons extra-virgin olive oil
2 brown onions, chopped
4 garlic cloves, chopped
2 tablespoons thyme leaves
2 tablespoons dried oregano
1 tablespoon ground cinnamon
¼ cup (60 g) tomato paste (concentrated purée)
2 kg (4 lb 8 oz) minced (ground) lamb
3 × 400 g (14 oz) tins diced tomatoes

WHITE SAUCE
50 g (1¾ oz) butter
2 brown onions, sliced
¼ cup (45 g) brown rice flour
4 cups (1 litre) full-cream milk
2 cups (200 g) grated cheddar, plus extra grated cheese for topping

Start by slow-cooking the onions for the white sauce. Heat the butter in a small saucepan over low heat and add the onion. Cook for 30 minutes, or until the onion has softened, stirring occasionally. Remove from the heat and set aside.

Preheat the oven to 180°C (350°F).

Place the eggplant slices on a baking tray lined with baking paper, drizzle with a little of the olive oil and season. Bake for 25–30 minutes, or until slightly softened, then remove from the oven and set aside.

Meanwhile, heat the remaining olive oil in a large saucepan or frying pan over medium heat. Add the onion and garlic and sauté for 4–5 minutes.

Add the herbs and cinnamon and stir. Add the tomato paste and cook for a further 2–3 minutes.

Turn the heat to high, add the mince and cook until well browned (or you can pre-brown the mince in batches in a separate frying pan), then add the tomatoes and season. Cook for another 30 minutes before removing from the heat.

Spoon enough mince mixture into a baking dish to evenly cover the base. Now add a layer of eggplant. Repeat the layers, finishing with a layer of eggplant. Refrigerate for 30 minutes.

Place the softened onion back over medium–low heat, add the flour and stir using a wooden spoon. Slowly add the milk, gently whisking as you go. Gradually add the cheese, whisking until it is well incorporated. Warm until the cheese has melted, then remove from the heat.

Blitz the mixture with a stick blender until smooth and combined.

Remove the baking dish from the fridge and gently pour the white sauce over the top. Sprinkle with extra grated cheese.

Place in the oven and bake for 30 minutes, or until the top is beautifully browned. Allow to cool slightly before serving.

Til's Vegetarian Lentil Cottage Pie

A very underrated dish, I reckon. Most meat eaters would probably turn their noses up at this, but it's full of flavour, easy to make and very filling. It's also my go-to when I have veggo friends coming for lunch or dinner, as Scott is sometimes at a loss in those scenarios.

SERVES 4

LENTIL FILLING
1 cup (215 g) green lentils,
   rinsed and drained
2 cups (500 ml) vegetable broth
2 tablespoons olive oil
1 onion, finely chopped
2 carrots, diced
2 celery stalks, diced
2 garlic cloves, finely chopped
1 teaspoon dried rosemary
1 teaspoon dried thyme
1 cup (130 g) frozen peas

MASHED CAULIFLOWER TOPPING
1 large head cauliflower,
   chopped into florets
2 tablespoons butter, or
   extra-virgin olive oil
1 cup (100 g) grated cheddar
   (optional)

In a saucepan, combine the lentils and vegetable broth. Bring to the boil, then reduce the heat and simmer for 20–25 minutes, or until the lentils are tender. Drain any excess liquid and set aside.

In a large frying pan, heat the olive oil over medium heat. Add the onion, carrot and celery and sauté for 5–7 minutes, or until the vegetables are softened.

Add the garlic and herbs and cook for another 1–2 minutes until fragrant.

Stir in the cooked lentils and frozen peas and season to taste. Cook for another 3–4 minutes, allowing the flavours to meld. Remove from the heat and set aside.

For the topping, steam the cauliflower until tender, about 8–10 minutes.

Transfer the steamed cauliflower to a food processor, add the butter and some salt and pepper, and blitz until smooth and creamy. Adjust the seasoning to taste.

Preheat the oven to 190°C (375°F).

Transfer the lentil filling to a baking dish, spreading it out evenly.

Carefully spoon the mashed cauliflower topping over the lentil filling. I like to use a fork to create decorative peaks on the surface when I'm feeling fancy.

Bake in the oven for 20–25 minutes, or until the edges are bubbling. If you're adding the cheese, sprinkle this over and pop back in the oven for a further 5 minutes, or until golden brown. Remove from the oven and let it cool slightly before serving.

Chicken Schnitzel with Charred Broccolini

Who doesn't love a chicken schnitty?! This is an archetypal Australian dish but with a gluten-free twist. You thought coconut flour was just for desserts? Think again.

SERVES 4

2 large eggs, beaten
1 cup (120 g) coconut flour,
    or besan (chickpea flour)
1 cup (65 g) shredded coconut
2 tablespoons chopped
    oregano
2 tablespoons chopped
    thyme leaves
2 chicken breast fillets,
    halved lengthways, at room
    temperature
4 tablespoons extra-virgin
    olive oil
1 tablespoon salted butter
bunch broccolini, trimmed
zest and juice of 1 lemon,
    to serve

HERB LEMON DRIZZLE
juice of 1 lemon
2 tablespoons extra-virgin
    olive oil
2 tablespoons chopped parsley

Beat the eggs in a wide, shallow bowl. Tip the flour onto a plate.

On another plate, combine the coconut, oregano and thyme.

Dip the chicken breast first in the flour, then in the egg, then press into the coconut mixture. Season with salt and pepper.

Heat 2 tablespoons of the olive oil over medium–high heat in a large frying pan.

Once hot, place the fillets in the pan (you may need to work in batches) and cook for 4–6 minutes, or until browned, before flipping over and cooking for 4–6 minutes on the other side. For the final 1–2 minutes of cooking, add the butter to finish browning the chicken.

Meanwhile, heat the remaining olive oil in another frying pan over high heat and add the broccolini. Cook for 8–10 minutes, or until nicely charred, then remove from the heat.

Once the chicken is cooked and nicely browned, remove from the heat and allow to rest for 4–5 minutes.

Meanwhile, mix together the ingredients for the herb lemon drizzle and season to taste.

Transfer the schnitzel to a serving plate, add some lemon zest and juice, and add the charred broccolini to the plate. Pour the herb lemon drizzle over the broccolini. Season and serve.

Chuck-eye Roast with Cowboy Butter and Roasted Parsnips

The chuck-eye roast comes from the chuck primal, which is located near the shoulder of the beast. It's adjacent to the rib-eye roast, but is usually more affordable, making it a pretty underrated but delicious cut. The cowboy butter is a great accompaniment – just add some pan-fired greens and you'll be in heaven.

SERVES 4–6

1 chuck-eye rolled fillet
4 tablespoons extra-virgin
  olive oil
4 parsnips, trimmed and
  quartered lengthways

COWBOY BUTTER
150 g (5½ oz) butter
2 eschalots, roughly chopped
¼ bunch parsley leaves
4 garlic cloves, peeled
3 tablespoons finely chopped
  chives
zest and juice of 1 lemon
1 teaspoon chilli flakes
1 teaspoon dijon mustard
1 teaspoon tahini

Remove the chuck-eye from the fridge 1 hour before cooking.

Preheat the oven to 165°C (325°F).

Heat 2 tablespoons of the olive oil in a frying pan over high heat. Generously season the beef and sear all sides in the pan until a deep brown crust develops.

Once entirely browned, transfer the beef to a baking tray and add the parsnip, drizzling the remaining olive oil over the parsnip. Season with salt and pepper.

Roast for around 1 hour, or until the internal temperature of the beef reaches 135°C (275°F) on a probe thermometer.

While the beef is cooking, place all the ingredients for the butter in a food processor or blender and blitz until combined. Season to taste and transfer to an airtight container. Any leftover butter will keep in the fridge for up to 1 month.

Once the beef is cooked, remove from the baking tray and place on a chopping board for 10 minutes to rest.

If the parsnips need a little longer, return them to the oven while the beef is resting.

After resting, carve the beef and serve with a generous dollop of butter and the roasted parsnips.

Ten-minute Kid-friendly Green Spaghetti

This dish was invented out of frustration when I couldn't get my kids to eat any greens, and pasta seemed to be the only thing they were interested in. 'Aha!' I thought, 'I'll outsmart you!' And guess, what? I did. (But also, I love this pasta sauce too so it's a win all round.)

SERVES 2

250 g (9 oz) uncooked
   gluten-free spaghetti, or
   pasta of your choice
1 head broccoli, cut into florets
1 cup (250 g) butter
1 cup (100 g) grated cheddar
½ cup (125 ml) full-cream milk

Bring a saucepan of salted water to the boil and cook the spaghetti according to the packet instructions, stirring often so it doesn't clump together.

Bring a medium saucepan of water to the boil and cook the broccoli until a fork easily slides through a floret. Drain and pop into a blender or food processor with the remaining ingredients. Blend on medium speed until smooth.

Drain the spaghetti and place in a bowl. Mix the green sauce through and serve.

sweets
and treats

Apple Crumble with Star Anise and Hemp

This delicious, warming apple crumble is a far cry from the English apple crumbles I was raised on in the UK. This version has been spiced up and the topping healthified with hemp seeds, which are rich in fatty acids, omega 3 and 6, and high in protein fibre. Plus, the coconut is rich in medium-chain triglycerides (MCTs) and antioxidants. Does it even qualify as a dessert?!

SERVES 10–12

APPLES

1.25 kg (2 lb 12 oz) apples, cored and cut into 3 cm (1¼ inch) wedges
2 tablespoons ground cinnamon
1 teaspoon ground star anise
1 teaspoon ground cardamon
½ teaspoon ground nutmeg
2 tablespoons coconut sugar

TOPPING

2–3 tablespoons coconut sugar, or sugar of your choice
2 cups (130 g) shredded coconut
1 cup (170 g) hemp seeds
1 cup (125 g) slivered almonds
1 tablespoon ground cinnamon
½ cup (125 g) salted butter, roughly chopped

Place the apple in a large mixing bowl and sprinkle the spices and coconut sugar over the top. Toss to ensure the apples are evenly coated.

Transfer to a saucepan with 300 ml (10½ fl oz) water, cover with a lid and place over low heat.

Leave the apples to stew gently for about 45 minutes, mixing every 10 minutes or so with a wooden spoon.

Meanwhile, make the topping by combining the sugar, coconut, hemp seeds, almonds and cinnamon and tossing together.

Add the butter and use your hands to rub it into the topping ingredients to form a crumb.

Preheat the oven to 150°C (300°F).

Once the apples have softened, remove the pan from the heat and transfer the apple mixture to a baking dish.

Sprinkle the topping over the apples and place in the oven for 15 minutes, or until the topping has browned.

Remove from the oven and enjoy with some home-made ice cream (see page 178).

Honey-roasted Stone Fruit with Vanilla Yoghurt

This delightful dessert celebrates the natural sweetness of seasonal stone fruits, enhanced by a drizzle of honey and a dollop of luscious vanilla yoghurt.

SERVES 4

4 tablespoons honey
2 tablespoons unsalted butter, or coconut oil, melted
1 teaspoon ground cinnamon
a pinch of salt
8–12 ripe stone fruits (peaches, nectarines, plums, or a mixture), halved and pitted
1 cup (260 g) Greek-style yoghurt
1 teaspoon vanilla extract

Preheat the oven to 200°C (400°F).

In a small bowl, combine the honey, melted butter, cinnamon and salt.

Arrange the halved and pitted stone fruit in a baking dish, cut side up.

Drizzle the honey mixture over the fruit, ensuring an even coating.

Bake in the oven for 15–20 minutes, or until tender and caramelised (the edges of the fruit should be slightly golden).

Meanwhile, whisk together the yoghurt and vanilla extract and set aside.

Once the fruit is deliciously golden, remove from the oven.

Serve with a generous dollop of vanilla yoghurt.

Nectarine and Berry Sorbet with Crushed Macadamia Nuts

Nectarine and berry sorbet, paired with the buttery richness of crushed macadamia nuts, is the perfect dessert when you're craving something both fresh and a little comforting. And it's so easy to prepare, it would be rude not to make it!

SERVES 4

4 nectarines, pitted and
  roughly chopped
150 g (5½ oz) mixed berries
  (strawberries, raspberries,
  blueberries)
¼ cup (90 g) honey, or
  maple syrup
1–2 tablespoons lemon juice
½ teaspoon vanilla extract
¼ cup (35 g) crushed
  macadamia nuts, to serve

In a blender or food processor, combine all the ingredients except the nuts and blitz until smooth. Taste the sorbet base and adjust the sweetness with more honey if needed.

Pour into a freezer-safe container and cover with a lid. Freeze for at least 4 hours, or until the sorbet is firm.

When the sorbet is ready, take it out of the freezer and let it sit at room temperature for a few minutes to soften slightly.

Once softened, scoop the sorbet into serving bowls or cones and top with the macadamias.

Richard's Bread 'n' Butter Pudding

My dad was a publican for 40 years and always had his head in a dog-eared cookbook looking for inspiration for daily specials or events. He had a few signature dishes, and his bread 'n' butter pudding was one of them.

SERVES 6

3–4 tablespoons unsalted butter, plus extra for greasing
6–8 slices of day-old gluten-free or sourdough bread, crusts removed
2 cups (300 g) diced peaches (optional)
3 large eggs
2 cups (500 ml) full-cream milk
½ cup (125 ml) thick (double) cream, plus extra to serve
¼ cup (45 g) coconut sugar, plus extra for sprinkling
1 teaspoon vanilla extract
1 teaspoon ground cinnamon
¼ teaspoon ground nutmeg
a pinch of salt
¼ cup (60 ml) Baileys Irish Cream
¼ cup (60 ml) Tia Maria

Grease a 23 × 23 cm (9 × 9 inch) baking dish with a little softened butter.

Butter each slice of bread on one side and cut into triangles.

Arrange half of the bread triangles, buttered side up, in a single layer in the bottom of the greased baking dish.

Sprinkle half of the peach (if using) evenly over the bread.

Place the remaining buttered bread triangles on top, creating another layer, then add the rest of the peach.

In a separate bowl, whisk together the eggs, milk, cream, sugar, vanilla, cinnamon, nutmeg and salt until well combined.

Add the Baileys and Tia Maria and whisk again.

Pour the custard mixture over the bread and fruit, ensuring all the bread is soaked with the custard. Gently press down on the bread with a spoon to help it absorb the custard.

Sprinkle some extra coconut sugar over the top to create a lovely golden crust when baked.

Preheat the oven to 175°C (325°F).

Cover the dish with foil and leave to stand for 20 minutes before baking in the oven for 30–40 minutes.

After 30 minutes, remove the foil and bake for a further 20–25 minutes, or until the top is golden and the custard is set.

Remove from the oven and allow to cool a little. Serve warm with dollops of cream.

Charred Pineapple with Lime-Coconut Cream and Toasted Coconut

Nothing says summer like pineapple! This dessert is the perfect way to end a warm evening. Does your mouth ever feel funny after eating pineapple? That's thanks to the enzyme bromelain, which breaks down proteins – and not just in food, the proteins in our mouths, too! Charring the pineapple decreases the bromelain content, making it perfect for those wanting to avoid the uncomfortable mouthfeel.

SERVES 4

2–3 tablespoons honey
1 teaspoon vanilla extract
1 cup (55 g) coconut flakes
1 ripe pineapple, trimmed
   and cut into thick wedges
   or slices
400 ml (14 fl oz) tin coconut
   cream, refrigerated
   overnight to chill
zest and juice of 1 lime

Preheat the barbecue or a chargrill pan to medium–high heat.

Mix together the honey and vanilla extract, then set aside.

Add the coconut flakes to a dry frying pan set over low heat and toast for a few minutes (don't walk away) until lightly golden. Remove from the heat and set aside.

Brush the pineapple with the honey mixture, ensuring it is evenly coated.

Place the pineapple on the barbecue or in the chargrill pan and cook for 2–3 minutes, turning regularly, or until well caramelised on both sides.

Meanwhile, remove the coconut cream from the fridge and open. Spoon the cream into a bowl, leaving behind the water. Add the lime zest and whisk until it stiffens, then set aside.

Once the pineapple has caramelised, remove from the heat and top with some toasted coconut flakes and a squeeze of lime juice. Serve the coconut cream alongside.

Tashi's Toast and Scott's Berry Butter

He may not know it yet, but Tashi is quite the cook. He's meticulous, takes his time, and aims for perfection. This includes his devotion to his French toast (one of his signature dishes) on the weekends. Interestingly, in France it's called 'pain perdu', which translates as 'lost bread' – a way of saving stale bread. In Spain, it's known as 'torrija', and in the UK, it's called 'eggy bread'. In our house it's Tashi's Toast.

SERVES 6

2 eggs, lightly beaten
a splash of milk
1 teaspoon extra-virgin olive oil
1 tablespoon butter
8–10 slices of gluten-free or
   sourdough bread

BERRY BUTTER
½ cup (40 g) blackberries
1 cup (150 g) strawberries
200 g (7 oz) salted butter
zest and juice of 1½ lemons
2 tablespoons coconut sugar

To make the butter, combine the berries in a bowl and mash with a fork until the juice and pulp have separated. Pour the mixture into a fine-mesh sieve and catch the juice in a bowl underneath. Set the juice aside.

Place the butter in a food processor and add the berry pulp, lemon zest and juice, and the sugar and blitz until combined. Transfer to an airtight container. It will keep for 2–3 days in the fridge.

In a bowl, lightly whisk the eggs and milk.

Heat the olive oil and butter in a frying pan over medium heat. Dip the bread into the egg and milk wash and, once the butter is foaming, place the bread in the pan. Fry on both sides until nicely browned.

Remove from the pan and add a dollop of the berry butter. Drizzle some of the berry juice over and scatter with fresh berries too, if you like.

Banana Bread

Call it bread, call it cake. But either way, call it delicious. Home-made banana bread is a no-brainer. It tastes 1000 per cent better than its shop-bought counterpart, and you can have it for breakfast, as a snack, or an evening treat – that's if it lasts that long. Ours never does.

SERVES 8

2 tablespoons salted butter
3 large ripe bananas, peeled
  and mashed
½ cup (100 g) coconut sugar
¼ cup (60 g) unsalted butter,
  melted
¼ cup (70 g) plain yoghurt
2 large eggs
1 teaspoon vanilla extract
1½ cups (150 g) almond meal
1 teaspoon baking powder
1 teaspoon ground cinnamon
¼ teaspoon ground nutmeg
a pinch of sea salt
¾ cup (90 g) chopped walnuts

Preheat the oven to 180°C (350°F). Grease a 23 × 13 cm (9 × 5 inch) loaf tin with the butter.

In a large mixing bowl combine the mashed banana, coconut sugar, melted butter, yoghurt, eggs and vanilla extract and mix well.

In a separate bowl, combine all the dry ingredients except the walnuts.

Gradually add the dry ingredients to the wet mixture, stirring gently until fully combined. Finally, fold in the chopped walnuts.

Pour the batter into the loaf tin and bake for 45 minutes, or until a skewer inserted in the middle of the loaf comes out clean. Remove from the oven and leave to cool in the tin for 10 minutes before turning out onto a wire rack to cool completely.

Slice and serve.

Blackberry Jam

My mum's favourite breakfast is jam on toast. We'd make it for her every Mother's Day. (I know, an easy win.) Here's our version, without the processed sugar. Instead, we've used maple syrup as a natural sweetener. (That doesn't make it sugar-free, mind you, but it's a vast improvement on the white stuff.)

MAKES 2 CUPS (640 G)

4 cups (520 g) fresh blackberries
½ cup (125 ml) maple syrup, or honey
2 tablespoons lemon juice
1–2 teaspoons lemon zest
1 teaspoon vanilla extract (optional)

Sterilise your glass jars and lids by placing them in a large pot of boiling water for 10 minutes. Remove and let them air-dry on a clean towel.

Wash the blackberries thoroughly under cold running water and remove any stems or leaves. Place the blackberries in a large, non-reactive stainless-steel saucepan and use a potato masher or the back of a fork to gently mash them. You can leave some small chunks for texture if you like.

Pour the maple syrup over the mashed blackberries, then add the lemon juice and lemon zest.

Place the saucepan over medium heat and bring the mixture to a simmer. Stir frequently to prevent burning or sticking. As the jam cooks, you may notice foam forming on the surface. Skim this off with a spoon and discard.

Let the mixture simmer for about 20–30 minutes, or until it thickens to your desired consistency. Remember that it will continue to thicken as it cools.

To test if the jam is ready, place a small amount on a cold plate or spoon and let it cool for a minute. Run your finger through it; if it wrinkles and holds its shape, it's ready.

If using, stir in the vanilla extract for extra flavour just before removing the jam from the heat.

Carefully ladle the hot jam into the sterilised jars, leaving about 5 mm (¼ inch) of space at the top. Wipe the rims clean with a damp cloth to ensure a good seal, then put on the lids. Let the jars cool to room temperature; they should seal as they cool. Any jars that don't seal can be refrigerated and consumed within a few weeks.

Once the jam has cooled and set, you can enjoy it on toast, pancakes and waffles, or as a topping for yoghurt or ice cream.

Salted Caramel and Honey No-churn Ice Cream

Not to sound like a total bore, but we make our own ice cream and sauce to avoid the additives, preservatives and food colourings that shop-bought ones are often laden with. Plus, it's a fun thing to do with the kids. This isn't an every-day-of-the-week event because we've found it really impacts the kids' interest in savoury food, so we try to keep it for special occasions. Making caramel can be quite tricky, but we've simplified that here too.

SERVES 6

SALTED CARAMEL SAUCE
1 cup (250 ml) maple syrup, or honey
6 tablespoons unsalted butter
½ cup (125 ml) thick (double) cream
1 teaspoon sea salt, or to taste

ICE-CREAM BASE
2 cups (500 ml) thick (double) cream
⅓ cup (115 g) honey
1 teaspoon vanilla extract
3 egg yolks

To make the salted caramel sauce, have all the ingredients ready to go because it can come together quickly.

Warm the maple syrup in a heavy-based saucepan over medium heat, stirring constantly until it becomes a deep amber colour and thickens slightly. This should take 5–7 minutes.

Once the maple syrup reaches the desired colour, add the butter all at once. Be careful; it will bubble up. Stir until the butter is completely melted and combined.

Slowly pour in the cream, stirring continuously. Be cautious as it may bubble up again if you pour too much in at once. Continue to cook and stir for another 1–2 minutes until the caramel is smooth and slightly thickened.

Remove the caramel sauce from the heat and stir in the sea salt. Taste and adjust the saltiness if necessary. Set aside to cool slightly, then transfer to an airtight container and place in the freezer for 20 minutes to chill and thicken.

In a mixing bowl, whip the cream until stiff peaks form, then place in the fridge to keep cool.

In a small saucepan set over low heat, melt the honey and mix in the vanilla extract.

Place the egg yolks in the bowl of a stand mixer and beat on high for 5 minutes. You can also use a mixing bowl and a handheld electric mixer for this. Slowly pour the honey mix into the beaten egg yolks. Continue beating until the mixture thickens, about 4–5 minutes.

Add the whipped cream and gently fold in, being careful not to deflate the cream too much.

Pour about half of the ice-cream mixture into a container. Drizzle one-quarter of the chilled salted caramel sauce over the ice cream.

Add the remaining ice cream mixture, then another one-quarter of the sauce. Use a knife or skewer to swirl the caramel through the ice cream to create a marbled effect.

Cover the container with a sheet of baking paper and freeze for at least 4–6 hours, or until the ice cream is firm.

Serve the extra caramel sauce on the side for pouring over the ice cream (like Ice Magic). This dessert is perfect with a side of berries.

Vegemite Butter Popcorn

This is the ultimate movie night accompaniment, especially for those who like their popcorn to come with a good dose of salty, umami flavour. And if you don't, we can't be friends.

SERVES 8

2 tablespoons coconut oil
½ cup (60 g) popcorn kernels

VEGEMITE BUTTER
½ cup (125 g) unsalted butter
1 tablespoon Vegemite

In a large pot with a tight-fitting lid, heat the coconut oil over medium heat.

Add one or two kernels to the pot, and if they pop, the oil is hot enough. Add the remaining kernels and cover with the lid.

Cook until the popping sound slows down and eventually stops, gently shaking the pot occasionally. Remove from the heat.

In a small saucepan, melt the butter over low heat, then add the Vegemite and stir until fully combined.

Drizzle the Vegemite butter over the popcorn and serve.

Frozen Berry and Granola Bliss

This recipe is the epitome of an evening at the Goodings'. In the small window of time we have to ourselves, Til and I will indulge in a dessert while cramming the new binge-worthy show ...

SERVES 2

1 cup (155 g) frozen blueberries
1 cup (260 g) plain yoghurt
zest of ½ lemon
2 teaspoons hemp oil
1 cup (90 g) Granola (page 38)

Get the berries out of the freezer 10 minutes before you plan to make this.

Add the yoghurt, berries and lemon zest to a blender and blitz for 5 seconds (some chunks are totally fine).

Pour into two serving bowls, drizzle with hemp seed oil and sprinkle with our granola. Enjoy!

Til's Gluten-free Dairy-free Ice-cream Sandwiches

I'm a big fan of dairy ice cream, but I found when I was breastfeeding Anouk that dairy didn't have a good effect on her little tummy, so I stopped consuming it for a good couple of months. Naturally, I had to find an ice-cream alternative, plus I needed the extra calories, so these bad boys fit the bill.

SERVES 4

BISCUITS
1 cup (100 g) almond meal
½ cup (75 g) coconut flour
¼ cup (20 g) shredded coconut
½ cup (55 g) cacao powder
a pinch of salt
¼ cup (90 g) honey, or
    maple syrup
½ cup (105 g) coconut oil,
    melted (you can also use
    MCT oil)
1 teaspoon vanilla extract

NO-CHURN ICE CREAM
2 × 400 ml (14 fl oz) tins full-fat
    coconut cream, refrigerated
    overnight to chill
½ cup (175 g) honey, or maple
    syrup
½ cup (110 g) coconut sugar
1 teaspoon vanilla extract

Line two 20 cm (8 inch) square cake tins with baking paper.

To make the biscuits, combine the almond meal, coconut flour, shredded coconut, cacao powder and salt in a bowl.

Add the honey, coconut oil and vanilla extract and mix until the dough comes together. If it's too dry, you can add more melted coconut oil until it feels soft enough to shape.

Divide the dough in half and press evenly over the base of the two tins. Chill while you prepare the ice cream.

Before you begin making the ice cream, make sure the coconut cream is well chilled. This allows the cream to separate from the liquid.

Open the tins and scoop out the cream, leaving the water behind. Place in a mixing bowl. (You can use the leftover water to make ice cubes. Simply pour into an ice-cube tray and freeze.)

Add the honey, coconut sugar and vanilla and whip the mixture until smooth and slightly fluffy.

Remove one tray of the biscuit from the fridge. Pour the ice-cream mixture on top and smooth out evenly. Freeze for 4 hours.

Remove the second biscuit from the fridge and carefully turn out of the tin. Place on top of the ice cream, pressing down gently. Freeze for another 2 hours.

Once the ice cream is firm, your dairy-free, gluten-free ice-cream sandwich biscuits are ready to enjoy! Simply remove from the freezer and cut into squares to serve, or slice like a cake.

staples

Salsa Verde

This is our life blood. It's salty, zesty, fresh and tangy. It's all the things. Best with steak, but great on just about anything – even eggs (see page 60). Yep, I said it.

MAKES 2 CUPS (500 ML)

1 garlic clove, peeled
2 long green chillies, destemmed
1 anchovy fillet
1 tablespoon capers, drained and rinsed
2 teaspoons dijon mustard
1 cup (250 ml) extra-virgin olive oil
1 cup (250 ml) white wine vinegar
¼ bunch mint leaves
1 bunch parsley stalks and leaves

Place all the ingredients in a blender with a good pinch of salt and pepper and blitz for 10–15 seconds, or until fully combined and vibrantly green.

Place in a glass jar and serve, or seal and store in the fridge for up to 2 weeks.

Note

If you have any ageing greens in the fridge, feel free to add these to your salsa. Just add to the blender with the rest of the ingredients and blitz until smooth.

Barbecue Sauce

Most commercial, shop-bought barbecue sauces should come with a health warning; they're full of sugar and preservatives. This sauce is better, and is one with great utility: perfect with a brisket, short ribs and full English breakfast. My dad used to pride himself on his barbecue sauce. I remember our family barbecues fondly ... the few we managed to have during our English 'summers'!

MAKES 400 ML (14 FL OZ)

2 tablespoons extra-virgin olive oil
4 garlic cloves, minced
2 eschalots, peeled and finely chopped
100 g (3½ oz) tomato paste (concentrated purée)
4–5 tablespoons honey
1 teaspoon sumac
½ teaspoon dried oregano
1 teaspoon smoked paprika
½ teaspoon sweet paprika
120 ml (4 fl oz) coconut aminos
    (teriyaki, otherwise regular is fine)
2 tablespoons dijon mustard

Heat the oil in a small saucepan over medium-low heat.

Add the garlic and eschalot and sauté for 5–6 minutes, or until softened.

Add the remaining ingredients with a good pinch of salt and pepper and stir well. Bring to a simmer and cook for another 5–10 minutes before removing from the heat.

Allow to cool. Either serve with your favourite slow-cooked meat or sausages.

The sauce will keep in an airtight container or bottle in the fridge for up to 2 weeks.

Spicy Romesco Sauce

Romesco sauce originated in the Catalonia region of Spain and was traditionally made with hazelnuts, but I love making it with macadamias for an Aussie twang. I also love to add some chilli for a little kick.

MAKES 1 CUP (250 ML)

2 large roasted red capsicums (peppers; shop-bought or home-made)
2 garlic cloves, peeled
200 g (7 oz) macadamia nuts, or hazelnuts
2 tablespoons tomato paste (concentrated purée)
2 teaspoons sweet paprika
2 tablespoons red wine vinegar
1 long red chilli, destemmed
¼ cup (60 ml) extra-virgin olive oil

Combine all the ingredients in a blender and blitz for 20–30 seconds, or until fully combined.

Store in an airtight container in the fridge for up to 1 month.

Lemon Mayonnaise

Knowing how to make mayonnaise is never a bad thing. Once you know the foundation you can add all sorts of other ingredients to customise it to particular dishes. The lemon zest and dill makes this a great mayo for salad, seafood and chicken.

MAKES 1½ CUPS (375 ML)

2 egg yolks
1 tablespoon dijon mustard
1 cup (250 ml) light olive oil, or avocado oil
zest and juice of 1 lemon
2 tablespoons finely chopped parsley
2 tablespoons finely chopped dill

In a mixing bowl, whisk together the egg yolks and dijon mustard until well combined and slightly creamy.

Gradually add the olive oil, drop by drop at first, while whisking vigorously. As the mixture begins to emulsify and thicken, you can gradually increase the stream of oil.

Continue whisking, adding enough oil to achieve a smooth, mayo-like consistency.

Once the mayo has formed, fold in the lemon zest and juice, parsley and dill.

Season and transfer to an airtight container. Store in the fridge for up to 2 weeks.

That Spicy Red Sauce

This is our version of that spicy red sauce people love to throw on just about anything. It's warming and fruity with just a hint of sweetness. And we've always got a jar of it on the go.

MAKES APPROX. 600 ML (21 FL OZ)

3 red capsicums (peppers), destemmed,
    cored and cut in half lengthways
300 g (10½ oz) cherry tomatoes, stalks removed
6 garlic cloves, peeled
1 tablespoon dried oregano
3 small red or green chillies, destemmed (use long
    chillies if you don't like too much spice)
130 ml (4½ fl oz) extra-virgin olive oil
1 tablespoon capers, drained and rinsed
4 anchovy fillets
50 ml (1¾ fl oz) white wine vinegar

Preheat the oven to 200°C (400°F).

Place the capsicum cheeks skin-side up in a roasting tin, then add the tomatoes, garlic, oregano, chillies and ⅓ cup (80 ml) of the olive oil. Season with salt and pepper and mix well to ensure everything is coated with the oil.

Roast for 30 minutes, or until the capsicum is nicely charred. Remove from the oven and allow to cool.

In a blender, place the capers, anchovies, vinegar and remaining olive oil. Lastly, add the contents of the roasting tin, being sure to pour all the delicious juices into the blender as well.

Blitz for 15 seconds, or until fully combined.

Season to taste before adding to absolutely anything.

Store any leftover sauce in an airtight container in the fridge for up to 1 month.

Tangy Lime Dressing

A great addition to some leafy greens and any protein that's slightly on the fatty side, such as salmon, chicken thigh or rump. Fatty foods can be intense in flavour, so a tart dressing – whether based on citrus or vinegar – can help balance the richness by providing a tangy contrast.

MAKES 100 ML (3½ FL OZ)

¼ cup (60 ml) extra-virgin olive oil
zest and juice of 1 lime
1 tablespoon apple cider vinegar, or white wine vinegar
2 teaspoons honey
1 teaspoon dijon mustard

Combine all the ingredients in a mixing bowl and whisk using a whisk or pop everything into a jar, secure with a lid and shake vigorously for 10 seconds.

Season to taste, then store in an airtight container in the fridge for up to 1 month.

Caramelised Onions

The key to caramelised onions is patience. Time is your best friend, so start them early and think low and slow. Gentle cooking with a bit of fat, like butter or oil, breaks down the natural sugars, caramelising the onion. This kind of magic simply can't be rushed.

MAKES 1½ CUPS (350 G)

2 tablespoons extra-virgin
  olive oil
1 tablespoon butter
4 large red onions, cut into
  1 cm (½ inch) slices
2 garlic cloves, crushed
2 teaspoons finely chopped
  thyme
1 tablespoon coconut sugar
2 tablespoons balsamic vinegar

Heat the oil and butter in a saucepan over medium heat and sauté the onion for 10 minutes.

Reduce the heat to low and add the remaining ingredients. Cook for 1 hour, stirring occasionally, until the onions are deeply caramelised and jammy.

Season lightly with salt and pepper, then remove from the heat. Store in an airtight container in the fridge for up to 2 weeks.

Black Olive Butter

Butter basically runs in our veins, and over the years I've experimented with so many flavour combinations. Butter is an ideal carrier for many herbs, spices and other flavourings. Adjust how much you blend this butter for different textures.

MAKES 175 G (6 OZ)

150 g (5½ oz) salted butter
2 garlic cloves, peeled
50 g (1¾ oz) black olives, pitted
2 anchovy fillets
¼ bunch fresh parsley

Combine all the ingredients in a food processor or blender and blitz for 20 seconds or until smooth.

Taste and adjust the seasoning, then transfer to an airtight container and store in the fridge for up to 1 month.

Chilli Sauce

Every kitchen should have a chilli sauce, chilli oil or chilli jam. As you've probably established reading these recipes, I enjoy spice and heat. I know that not everyone does, so tweak this according to your taste by using different chillies to turn the heat up or down. Try anaheim or poblano chillies for something milder, or go for habaneros or Serranos if you are a heat seeker.

MAKES 1½ CUPS (375 ML)

2 tablespoons coconut oil
10–12 red jalapeño chillies, destemmed and
  roughly chopped
1 small onion, roughly chopped
4 garlic cloves, roughly chopped
1 cm (½ inch) piece ginger, peeled and chopped
2 tablespoons white vinegar
1 tablespoon honey
1 teaspoon tamari
½ teaspoon paprika

Heat the coconut oil in a frying pan over medium heat and add the chilli, onion, garlic and ginger. Stir until thoroughly combined and the onion is translucent, about 8–10 minutes.

Pour in the vinegar, honey and tamari and stir. Add the paprika and stir again, then reduce the heat to low and cook for a further 10 minutes.

Remove from the heat and allow to cool.

Transfer to a food processor or blender and blitz until smooth. Taste and adjust the flavour with tamari, honey or vinegar if necessary.

Transfer to an airtight container and store in the fridge for up to 1 month. Serve with everything!

A message of hope from Rachel

My inspiration for transitioning my farm to regenerative practices and making the documentary *Rachel's Farm* came after personally experiencing the Australian Black Summer bushfires in 2019. As everyone agreed at the time, this was more than a bushfire. We had tipped into a long drought, but the burning of fossil fuels and bad land and forest management that had brought it on was our own making.

Like many, I was consumed by the despair that we would never right the wrongs we had created. My anxiety was heightened further by the arrival of grandchildren who would have to live with our generation's choices and practices.

I subsequently read Charles Massy's *Call of the Reed Warbler*, which details the challenges and accomplishments of many early adopters of the regenerative way of farming, and I was immediately filled with renewed hope. He talked about how we could regenerate the land, the soil, the nutrient and water cycle, and pull carbon from the air back into the soil with a different paradigm of land management. Namely, working with nature rather than dominating her.

In the short time that I have been farming regeneratively, and doing my homework, I have come to understand that the competition between retailers to push prices lower and lower is only made possible when the health of our food and our environment is not factored into the price. Perhaps you already understand this, but I shudder at how ignorant I was and how many still are: unwittingly playing a part in the degeneration of our health and landscapes, and polluting our waterways.

Of course, many, many farmers do their best. They don't want to see their soil degraded, their water tables shrinking and their rivers polluted with chemicals, but to stay both domestically and internationally competitive, what choice do they have? To put it into context, we are still living in a farming era that began in the 1970s when President Nixon's agricultural minister, Earl Butz, said 'Get big or get out'.

> Today, it is almost impossible for small farms to compete with industrial farms, their economies of scale and their lack of environmental considerations. The decline of the small family farm is evident everywhere.

But is this really what we want for our future? Are we okay with the rapid decline in our health, and the health of our landscapes, and the mental health of farmers battling to stay afloat on the ever-smaller returns for their labour? Are we okay with the city–country divide getting wider and wider, keeping us ignorant of the true cost of our cheap food until it's too late, when our small farms are gone, our soils are blown away, our food is empty of nutrition, and our rural towns are hollowed out?

My regenerative farming story is just one and I'm still learning, but I've subsequently met and read about hundreds of regenerative and organic farmers who are finding ways to scale up and increase productivity, all the while healing our wounded country, caring humanely for animals, and delivering the kind of healthy, tasty produce that our grandparents once enjoyed.

My hope for my film was that it would help fill the void between the food that sits on our plate and all the processes by which it got there. That it would illuminate the impact of different approaches to farming, and allow consumers to connect their food with their values.

Call me an idealist, or deluded, but I believe that it is only a question of filling in that blank behind the plate and many consumers will make the choice for their health, for flavour, for their children, their environment and their rural communities. And, of course, once consumers demand it in louder and louder voices, the retailers will rush to provide it, and everyone will breathe a sigh of relief as the planet makes a gentle shift towards hopefulness.

RACHEL WARD

NOW STREAMING ON STAN

POSTER © WILDBEAR ENTERTAINMENT PTY LTD AND NEW TOWN FILMS PTY LTD

Resources

Beermullah Beef A family-owned Red Angus beef farm located about 100 kilometres north of Perth around the beautiful Beermullah Lake. It sits within the Swan Coastal Plains and, with careful management, is slowly regenerating wetlands and biodiversity. beerrmullah.com.au | @beermullahbeef

Bundurra Farm and Butchery A true free-range pig farm, Bundurra choose not to farm conventionally and instead use biodynamic preparations on the soil, avoiding antibiotics and chemicals. They have adapted regenerative practices, resting the land to rejuvenate the grasses that naturally grow, and protecting the soil. farmingforgood.com.au | @bundarra_farm

Charlie Arnott A beautiful farm in Boorowa, NSW, producing beef, lamb and pigs, and managed using organic, biodynamic and holistic grazing principles. Charlie also runs biodynamic workshops, has a farm stay and produces a podcast called The Regenerative Journey in which he interviews people in the regen' space (Scott included). @charliearnott1 | charliearnott.com.au

Ethical Farmers A lush farm in Dungog producing food the way nature intended through regenerative and sustainable farming practices. @theethicalfarmers | ethicalfarmers.com.au

Fat Pig Farm A regenerative farm owned by Matthew Evans and located in southern Tasmania. Home to pigs, goats, bees, ducks and cows. @fat_pig_farm | fatpig.farm

Feather and Bone A fantastic butcher shop specialising in organic, regenerative and ethically raised meat with two NSW locations: Marrickville and Waverley. @featherandboneprovidore | featherandbone.com.au

Full Circle Farm A pasture-based regenerative farm located in the Dooralong Valley on the NSW Central Coast. They produce chemical-free eggs, beef and pork, and have a butcher shop called Full Circle Butchery in East Gosford. @fullcirclefarm_ | fullcirclefarm.com.au or fullcirclebutchery.com.au

Golden Hill Farm Regeneratively farmed meat chickens. Golden Hill are continuously learning how to increase the nutrient density of their chickens while improving the soil health and rejuvenating their pastures. goldenhillfarm.com.au | @goldenhill_farm

Goodies Farm A family-owned-and-operated mixed broadacre farm based in Kendenup, Western Australia. It is on a mission to improve soil health while providing food for its local community. goodiesfarm.com.au | @goodiesfarm

Integrity Meats A butcher shop in Goulburn, NSW, dedicated to providing nutrient-dense, chemical-free produce. @integritymeatsaustralia | integritymeats.com.au

K2 Farm A family- and community-run farm in the Adelaide Hills, South Australia. Working alongside local farmers to develop an on-farm ecosystem that integrates landscape rehabilitation and biodiversification with ethical, sustainable food and resource production. K2beef.com.au | @k2regenfarm

Levenvale Farm Grass-fed and grass-finished beef grown on a certified organic farm in Bellingen, NSW, using regenerative principles. @bellingenbeef | levenvalefarm.com.au

Lomandra Farm A small-scale, chemical-free market garden on Dhudhuroa Country in Victoria's north-east. They take great pride in the quality, freshness and tastiness of their veggies. lomandrafarm.com | @lomandra_farm

Macintyre Brook Lamb Located in Queensland's Western Downs region, Macintyre Brook Lamb is the realisation of one family's dream to provide consumers with a nutritious and delicious protein produced with a strong environmental conscience. macintyrebrookfarm.com.au | @macintyrebrooklamb

Miller + Baker A family-owned-and-run flour mill and bakery located in one of the friendliest neighbourhoods in Perth, Western Australia. They source their grain from Western Australian farmers – specifically, from farmers dedicated to improving soil biology. millerandbaker.com.au | @millerandbaker

Misty Creek Agroforestry A chicken, egg and flower farm located in the Northern Rivers of NSW, using syntropic farming and holistic management techniques. @mistycreek.agroforestry

Moonrise Seaweed Co. are developing a small-scale seaweed farming system suited to the Australian environment under First Nations guidance. moonriseseaweed.farm | @moonriseseaweedco

Morelands Lamb A sheep and lamb farm for more than 160 years. Today, the legacy continues using a combination of biodynamic and regenerative farming techniques. moorlands lamb.com.au

Oranje Tractor Wine is a small regenerative vineyard, eco-orchard and tasting room in Albany, Western Australia. They were certified organic from 2005 to 2021, and are now focused on implementing regenerative agriculture practices and educating others. oranjetractor.com.au | @oranjetractorfarm

Tathra Place A regenerative multi-species farm in Wombeyan Caves, NSW. Chemical-free, pasture-raised beef, pork, lamb, duck and quail. Order direct from the farm and get your produce delivered to your door. @tathraplace | tathraplacefreerange.com

The Food Farm Regeneratively farmed organic chicken and grass-fed beef on the Central Coast of NSW. Delivering to doors across the state. @thefoodfarmau

WATCH
The Biggest Little Farm on Apple TV
Common Ground on Prime Video
Kiss the Ground on Netflix
Rachel's Farm on Stan

READ
Call of the Reed Warbler by Charles Massy
Farm by Nicola Harvey
Soil by Matthew Evans
*Why You Should Give a F*ck about Farming* by Gabrielle Chan

Acknowledgements

TIL

To my dad. Thanks for cheering us on, but also asking the hard questions. You are (so annoyingly) (almost) always right. To my mum. Thanks for chewing our ears off about regen' and consequently changing the course of my life. And for making the farm even more magical than it already was. I love you both to infinity and beyond.

To my husband. Thank you for putting up with my endless bossing. No one could ever live with me and work with me, except someone with as much patience and good humour as you.

SCOTT

I owe much of this book and The Good Farm Shop to my parents. Firstly, for never doubting my pursuits but, secondly and more importantly, for giving me the inspiration for the dishes I cook today. I owe my fervour for food to growing up in their pubs and absorbing ideas and techniques by osmosis. I would also like to acknowledge my other parents (my in-laws) for their unwavering support, love and for quizzing my ideas, which always paves the way for better ideas. Thank you!

TOGETHER

Thank you to Jane Novak, our agent, who first appeared as a loyal customer, and then, through following our socials and reading our newsletters, saw something more – a Good Farm book.

To Jane Willson, our publisher at Murdoch. For finding our original submission buried under a pile of other submissions, giving it CPR and bringing it to life. Thank you to the team behind the scenes: Loran McDougall, Virginia Birch, Andrea O'Connor, Sarah Odgers, Lucy Sykes-Thompson, Madeleine Kane, Eugenie Baulch, Max McMaster, Lou Playfair, Sarah Hatton. Special thanks to Cath Muscat and David Morgan for creating such beautiful food images, and possibly the hardest job of all … thank you to our home economy team, Kerrie Worner and Tammi Kwok.

And lastly to our kids, who can't even read. Thanks for still calling us mum and dad after a year of us building a food business and writing a cookbook, which ironically meant that sometimes we forgot to feed you.

Index

Published in 2024 by Murdoch Books, an imprint of Allen & Unwin

Murdoch Books Australia
Cammeraygal Country
83 Alexander Street
Crows Nest NSW 2065
Phone: +61 (0)2 8425 0100
murdochbooks.com.au
info@murdochbooks.com.au

Murdoch Books UK
Ormond House
26–27 Boswell Street
London WC1N 3JZ
Phone: +44 (0) 20 8785 5995
murdochbooks.co.uk
info@murdochbooks.co.uk

For corporate orders and custom publishing, contact our business development team
at salesenquiries@murdochbooks.com.au

Publisher: Jane Willson
Editorial managers: Virginia Birch, Loran McDougall
Design manager: Sarah Odgers
Concept designer: Studio Polka
Designer: Madeleine Kane
Editor: Andrea O'Connor @ Asterisk & Octopus
Photographer: Cath Muscat
Stylist: David Morgan
Home economists: Kerrie Worner, Tammi Kwok
Production director: Lou Playfair

ISBN 978 1 76150 022 0

 A catalogue record for this
book is available from the
National Library of Australia

A catalogue record for this book is available from the British Library

Colour reproduction by Splitting Image Colour Studio Pty Ltd, Wantirna, Victoria
Printed by C&C Offset Printing Co. Ltd., China

OVEN GUIDE: You may find cooking times vary depending on the oven you are using. For fan-forced
ovens, as a general rule, set the oven temperature to 20°C (35°F) lower than indicated in the recipe.

TABLESPOON MEASURES: We have used 20 ml (4 teaspoon) tablespoon measures. If you are using a
15 ml (3 teaspoon) tablespoon add an extra teaspoon of the ingredient for each tablespoon specified.

10 9 8 7 6 5 4 3 2 1

'A clarion call to live a life of regeneration and hope, to fill our bellies with fine food while restoring and repairing the earth.'
JULIA BAIRD, JOURNALIST, AUTHOR

'The Good Farm Shop makes saving the planet healthy and delicious!'
DAMON GAMEAU, ACTOR, DIRECTOR, PRODUCER

'I can feel, see and taste vitality, joy and confidence in Til and Scott's intuitive, generous, home-style cooking. Learning about their compelling individual journeys with food only deepens the flavour and character of these delicious recipes: humble, soulful cooking with a potent social, environmental and community purpose.'
KYLIE KWONG, CHEF, RESTAURATEUR, AUTHOR